Cut From The Same Cloth

Laura Lea

God is always with you!

Laura Lea
'05

Copyright©2005 Laura Lea
All characters in this book are fictitious. Any resemblance to actual persons,
living or dead, is purely coincidental.

All rights reserved
This book is protected under the copyright laws of the United States of America. Any
reproduction or unauthorized use of the material or artwork contained
herein is prohibited without the express
written permission of Laura Lea.
Distributed in the United States by The Author's Press.

No part of this book may be reproduced or transmitted in any form by any means,
electronic or mechanical, including photocopying and recording, or by any information
storage or retrieval system, except as may be expressly permitted in
writing from the publisher.
Requests for permission should be addressed to Laura Lea c/o The Author's Press.

Cover Art by Angela Taylor
Layout and Design by The Author's Press
First Printing: July 2005

Library of Congress Catalog Card: Pending

US ISBN: 1-933505-03-6

All Rights Reserved.

The distribution, scanning, and uploading of this information via the Internet or via any
other means without the permission of the publisher is illegal and
punishable by law.

Please contact The Author's Press to purchase authorized electronic editions.
Do not participate in or encourage piracy of copyrighted materials.

Your support of the author's rights is appreciated.

Cut From The Same Cloth

The Author's Press
Atlanta Aberdeen Los Angeles

Dedication

To my children, Emily, Amy, Benjamin and John, together you make up the heart and soul of Sam. It was a sweet experience to include you in this story, but, more importantly, an honor to have you as a part of mine.

And to their father, my husband, Buzz, thank you for encouraging this dream, and for watching over our nest so that I could be free to fly for a while.

Acknowledgements

In loving memory of my grandmother, Olene Gresham.

To my family and friends, thank you for listening to me talk about Sam and Gommy during the last fourteen months. I needed them to be real and you welcomed them as if they were family.

To my editor, H. Christine Lindblom, thank you for believing in my ability and pushing me through the process. I am a story teller and I can't wait to do it again.

To my comrades at Brewberries, thank you for taking this trip with me. Here's to *Coffee and a Story*.

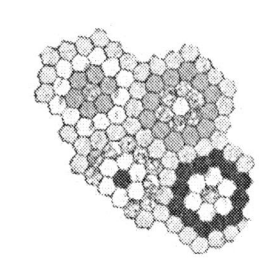

Chapter 1
Safety from the Storm

Sam lay perfectly still holding the covers tightly over her head, but it was no use. She couldn't muffle the loud claps of thunder. Stuffing her fingers in her ears and holding her pillow over her head did nothing to diminish the rattling booms. Just outside her bedroom window, nature's fireworks were in full swing. A part of her wanted to peel the covers back so that she could catch the fleeting views of marbleized sky. Lightning had always been her favorite part of a storm. The sight of silent, white hot, veins streaking through the starless night reminded her of the Fourth of July. The loud claps that usually followed were another story.

Still hiding beneath her covers, she wondered what it was about the sounds of the storm that made her heart pound. She had always loved fireworks. How could this be any different?

Come on, Sam, think fireworks, think Fourth of July, you ninny.

Cut from the Same Cloth

"Baaawk, bawk, bawk, bawk, baaawk," she squawked from under her downy hideaway.
Come on, you're inside, the storm's outside.
Just as she was about to throw back the covers, the empty space around her face began to glow, fading to black after only a second. The same familiar dread grabbed her so tightly, she could barely breathe. Trying to keep herself focused on the imminent thunder, she counted softly while huddled beneath her covers.
"One, one-thousand, two, one-thousand, three, one-thou—,"
Booboomboom.
Flattened against her mattress, Sam waited for the vibrating air to shake her bedroom. She would have preferred to wait in silence, but this had not been her lucky day. Even as the thunder rolled passed her house, the wind was preparing to take center stage. Howling with laughter, it pelted her window with pea sized bits of frozen rain.
Blasted wind, she thought.
Sam wanted desperately to overcome this paralyzing fear. Was it possible that her imagination was getting the best of her? The rapping continued on her window, tempting her to peek. After all, what if a frightened squirrel needed a safe place to weather the storm? Lying there with covers battened down around her, she could feel the beads of sweat gathering on her face.
Whew, it's getting hot under here.
Suffocating in the stifling heat, she would need to surface soon, storm or no storm. Listening to the wind as it howled passed her bedroom, she crossed fingers on both hands hoping this was its final pass.

Laura Lea

If she was lucky it would move on, content to chase the lightning and thunder.
   Just when she thought she couldn't bear her confinement any longer, she realized the haunting sounds were no longer blaring in her ears. The only noise she could hear now was the deafening sound of her pounding heart. Not about to wait for the storm's encore, she flung the covers so hard they flew onto the floor.
   "That's it," she said aloud. "I'm outta here."

✦ ✧ ✦

   *S*pringing from her bed, she lunged for the door.
   "Teddy," she shrieked. Without hesitation, she turned, leaped back onto her bed, grabbed her favorite bear, and in half a second, was standing in the long rectangle of pale, pink light that spilled from her grandmother's room. As if she had been holding her breath for quite awhile, she let out a long, deliberate sigh.
   Finally, her heart was finding its normal rhythm. Just knowing that her favorite person in the whole world was resting on the other side of the door made her feel safe. Peeking through the open space between the door and its frame, she caught a glimpse of her grandmother leaning back on the pillow she had propped against her headboard. Her petunia pink bifocal glasses balanced on the tip of her slightly upturned nose, while her paperback novel rested open on her chest.

Cut from the Same Cloth

"Gommy?" Sam whispered, not wanting to wake her grandmother if she was sleeping. "You still awake?"

"Hun-h, what?...oh," Gommy said, obviously startled from a deep sleep.

"Must have dozed off. I was trying to wait up for you. What took you so long?" Gommy asked, as she tossed the empty tissue box from her night stand into the waste can beside her bed.

Sitting herself up a little straighter, she closed her book and placed it in the night stand's bottom drawer.

"That's some storm out there. I tried to sleep, but the thunder kept waking me up. Thought I might read for a whi—."

Hachoo.

"Sam, honey, could you get me that tissue box?" she said, pointing to the chest over by the window. "I can't seem to get rid of this old cold."

Patting the bed, she motioned for Sam to join her. Sam grabbed the lavender box and turned back toward the bed.

The old, white, iron bed sat high off the floor making it necessary for Sam to get a running start in order to climb onto it safely. Two steps and both she and Teddy were airborne. Landing squarely, she grabbed the rail at the head of the bed and waited for the waves of motion to cease.

Even though she had never jumped on a real trampoline, she imagined it must be a lot like jumping on the iron bed. After all, they both sat high off the floor and had metal springs. Unable to help herself, she got on her knees and began to bounce.

Uurh-urh-uurh-urh...uurh-urh, the springs squealed with delight each time her knees struck the mattress.

Laura Lea

Before she knew it, Teddy had joined in the fun. Together they bounced, arms reaching higher with each upward climb. After four or five tries, Sam decided that even if she could reach the fan's pull chain, it was probably not a good idea to grab it. Totally exhausted and dripping with sweat, she and her playmate collapsed onto Gommy's quilt.

"Did you two finally wear yourselves out?"

"Teddy and I are hot." Sam sighed, wiping the moisture from her head with the tail of her night shirt.

"Gommy, do you think you could help me put a fan up in my room?"

"Mmmm, I'm not sure that's a good idea," Gommy said, cutting her eyes toward Sam, the corners of her mouth curling down into a smirk. "Maybe we should wait 'til you outgrow your bouncing phase."

They both grinned.

"Pardon me," Gommy said, trying hard to swallow down a cough.

Before it could reach the back of her throat, her mouth flew open and she coughed several times as though she was trying to dislodge a bone from the back of her throat. Instinctively, she grabbed a tissue and covered her mouth to keep the germs from spraying Sam.

"Wish I could get this old stuff to come up," she said when the coughing fit was over. "Know I'd feel better if I could."

Sam didn't believe for a minute that the storm was finished wreaking havoc. Yet, there was an eerie calmness settling over their house. Maybe the storm had wasted enough time bullying Providence and was

Cut from the Same Cloth

now rolling on in search of another unsuspecting town.

With the storm's snaps, crackles and pops off in the distance, Sam was anxious for the silence. Surprisingly, there was none.

She had been so preoccupied with the storm's rant, the whirling ceiling fan's ruckus had gone unnoticed. At least, this time she wasn't afraid. There would be no surprises, just the soft clicking sound of the pull chain as it tapped the fan's light globe in response to the vibration of the blades. Sam stared at the dangling chain, letting its swinging motion lull her into a trance. As the whirling blades stirred the air above her, the cool breeze blew across her sweat soaked night shirt.

"I'm cold, Gommy," she said, wrapping her arms around her chest hoping to make the chill bumps disappear.

"Crawl under here beside me," Gommy invited, folding her Flower Garden quilt back to give Sam room to scoot in beside her.

"You know, Sam, you don't ever have to be afraid, God's always with you."

"Hey, Gommy, you say that all the time."

"Just don't want you to forget," Gommy said, tapping Sam's nose with her index finger.

"It's been quiet for a while now, storms more'n likely passed us by. Guess you better head back to your room so's you can get to bed."

Turning toward her bed side table, Gommy glanced at the clock radio.

"Whew, it's past ten."

"Are you sure you don't need me to stay in here with you?" Sam said, as if she were fishing for an invitation.

Laura Lea

"I don't know about leaving you alone. Mom won't be back till midnight, what if you need something before then, and I don't hear you call my name?"
 Finally catching on to Sam's intentions, Gommy pretended that Sam was right.
 "You know what, I think you're right. Why don't you just sleep in here with me tonight?"
 "Yea," Sam yelled, throwing Teddy so high his ear hit the spinning fan blade.
 Eyeing her grandmother, Sam realized Gommy was peering suspiciously over the tops of her glasses.
 "Well," Sam said calmly, "I guess Teddy and I can stay, if you think you need us."
 For a few seconds Sam and Teddy wiggled and slid around on the bed trying to arrange their pillows. Snuggling under the old, worn, Flower Garden quilt with her grandmother and Teddy, she was instantly warmed, but not the least bit sleepy.
 "Hey, Gommy, I'm not sleepy yet. Can we stay up for a little while?"
 "Well, it's pretty late, don't you think we should turn out the light?"
 "No, just a little longer, *pleease, pleeeease,*" she begged. "Hey, I know, you can tell me about one of your quilt strips. Start with the part where Mee-Maw made your baby quilt with rags. I can't remember what comes after that."
 "Samantha Louise, there aren't too many of these quilt pieces that I haven't already told you about. You know this quilt almost as good as I do."
 "Oh, I know, but tell me again. Hey, show me your baby quilt."

Cut from the Same Cloth

"Well, I guess we have time for one story, but that's all. Just one, and then I'm turning off the light. I'm tired, you've kept me up past my bed time.
"All right," Sam sighed.
"Well, let me think," Gommy said.

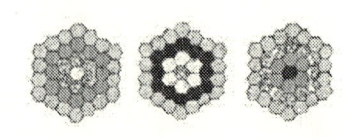

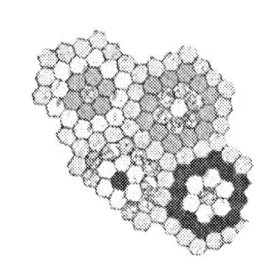

Chapter 2
A Piece from the Past

"I got my first quilt when I was a—."

"No, Gommy, go back to the part about Mee-Maw and the rag bag."

"Your great grandmother?"

"Amanda, right?" Sam said, proud that she had remembered her great-grandmother's name.

"I thought you didn't remember this story?" Gommy questioned.

"Oh, that was a lucky guess. Please keep going."

They exchanged glances. Each wearing a noticeable smirk.

"Well, we didn't have a lot of money, so Momma—"

"Gommy, were you poor?" Sam interrupted.

"No, not exactly, I mean...we didn't have much extra money, but we always had what we needed. I guess it never occurred to me that we might be poor. Anyway, do you remember when I told you about how Momma took my baby quilt and added strips to it?"

Cut from the Same Cloth

"Uh-huh."

"Good Lord, Sam, I can't remember what parts of this quilt we've already talked about. Did I tell you about my other strips?" Gommy asked, as her knotty index finger traced the seams that lay directly in front of her.

"Some of them. I think it's pretty neat that your momma kept adding strips. It's sorta like your quilt grew up with you. Hey, Gommy, here's Mom's strip." Sam said, pointing to the end strip whose colors were still bright enough to show the pattern on the fabric.

"Boy, she used to wear some loud clothes. When did she trade the color for the black and white stuff she wears now? I can't picture Mom wearing anything made from this stuff."

Sam stared for a long time at all of the colorful hexagons that her grandmother and her great grandmother had sewn together to make the Flower Garden quilt. Allowing her finger tips to move from piece to piece, she was surprised at their many textures.

"I sure am glad I went ahead and added your momma's strip when I did. When I get to feeling better, I'm gonna get to sewing on your strip. I don't lack much finishing the piecing on it, then it'll be ready to add on here with the rest of them. Just think, once that's done I'll have a quilt full of memories. All these pieces tell a story about someone in our family. Now you know why dreams are sweet when you sleep under a quilt."

Sam's mood suddenly darkened.

"Gommy, everybody's part of your quilt except for my—," she said turning away.

10

Laura Lea

Realizing that Sam was missing her daddy, Gommy revealed a secret that even Sam's mother didn't know.

"Look here, Sam. I have a special piece of fabric I haven't told you about yet."

Sam turned back towards the quilt, and sighed deeply. "Which one?"

"Hum, let me see if I can find it," Gommy said, straightening her bifocals.

"I know it's here somewhere," she said, continuing to trace the fabric hexagons in search of the piece in question. "Here it is," Gommy announced, pointing to a faded red and blue plaid flannel.

"What's so special about this one?" Sam asked.

"Well, it's a piece from one of your daddy's shirts."

Stunned, Sam didn't know what to say. She placed her right hand on the fabric. It was soft and thin. "You mean my daddy used to wear this? How did you get one of his shirts?"

"Well, after he died, your mother took some of his clothes over to the thrift store at *Bread of Life*. I guess this shirt ended up in my rag bag by mistake.

"You know, your daddy used to wear flannel shirts all the time, even in the summer. It'd be ninety degrees outside, and Peter would be mowing the lawn in a flannel shirt. Your momma and I would just shake our heads. There was no point in trying to get him to put on something cooler. He was a tad bit stubborn, you know.

"Hey, now I know who it is that you remind me of," Gommy said, smiling over at her granddaughter.

They both sat still for a few minutes, each lost in their own thoughts. Sam, trying to dress the young man in the picture on Gommy's dresser, in a red and blue plaid flannel shirt, and Gommy remembering a

Cut from the Same Cloth

simple, black shirt with a white square in the center of its collar.

All at once Gommy turned away, suddenly seized by a coughing fit. Quietly, Sam waited for the coughing to stop and for her grandmother to settle back under the covers. It seemed to her that Gommy had been sick forever. The cough started out as a cold in mid-winter and, though she had done everything her doctor had recommended, she had not been able to shake it. Instead, she had only gotten worse.

"Now, where were we before that fit hit me?" Gommy asked as if she was starting to tire.

"You were showing me my daddy's shirt." After a moment of silence, Sam gathered her courage and asked Gommy another question.

"Gommy, do you think there might be another one of my daddy's shirts in the rag bag?"

"Oh, I can't remember. I s'pose there might be. I'll look tomorrow. You want to keep it if I find one?"

"Could I? I mean do you think Mom would mind?"

"It's alright with me as long as you promise not to wear it when it's hot outside."

"Hey, Gommy, what about Mom's dad? Are there any patches from his clothes on here?" Sam asked as if she wasn't sure it was okay to bring up the subject.

"There's only one, hon. See that black ring with the yellow center. Well, that was his. He wore a lot of black."

"Black?" Sam asked. "How depressing."

"Well, I guess you could say it was part of his work clothes."

"Oh, well, I guess that's different. I mean, if he had to wear it for work, then he had to wear it for work."

Laura Lea

Gommy got really quiet, losing herself in her thoughts. Sam had asked questions about her mother's father before, but no one ever wanted to talk about him. All Sam knew was that he left Providence when her mother was four and that he died of cancer just before her mother turned twenty-four.

Just like her own father, there was rarely any mention of him, and his picture wasn't part of the collection of photos that graced the top of the old mahogany upright piano. What was it with her family and daddies? For some reason, the two didn't seem to go together very well.

"I'm pooped," Gommy said, reaching for the Victorian lamp that sat on the bedside table. "If I tried real hard I might sleep 'til noon tomorrow. You and Teddy can stay in here with me if you want to, but I'm going to sleep."

With that Gommy turned onto her left side, pulled her quilt up to her neck, then began her nightly snore fest.

Lying in the darkness between her grandmother and Teddy, Sam was asleep in minutes.

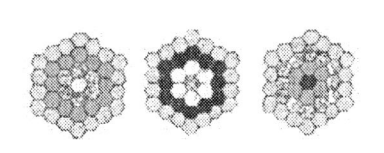

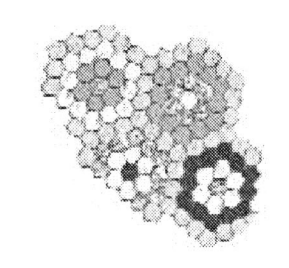

Chapter 3
The Bus Route

From the back of bus number eighty-two, Sam watched as the two-story, red brick courthouse zoomed past her window.

Riding the bus had always been one of her favorite parts of the school day. Every trip was different, with surprises around every corner. Never knowing what to expect, she peered anxiously through the dirty glass rectangle that eagerly waited to show her the world, or at the very least, Hamden County.

Why her friends didn't share her enthusiasm was difficult to understand. As far as she was concerned, being chauffeured from home to school and back home again in a yellow Blue Bird five days a week was awesome. To Sam's way of thinking, it was two, thirty minute chunks of her day when she was free to let her mind roam.

In a matter of seconds, she could soar over an open pasture, an eagle in search of an unsuspecting field mouse. With a wardrobe change, she could slip

Cut from the Same Cloth

into a leotard and swing herself onto the trapeze platform.

From there, a short climb would take her to the high wire. A healthy fear of heights would keep her from looking down. In a tremendous show of strength, she would effortlessly perform her gymnastics routine.

It would even be possible for her to gallop through the seven seas, riding bare back on a tiny sea horse in search of the lost city of *Atlantis*.

Sam knew that there were people who thought she had an overactive imagination, and maybe she did. Yet, she wasn't about to waste a single second fretting over the opinions of others. To her, the short trips she took in her mind were nothing more than intellectual excursions, quick vacations from the realities of living with a self-absorbed mother.

Making her way through the streets of Providence on her way to the only elementary school, her chauffeur, Miss Molly, eased the bus through the intersection of Little River Road and Steele Court.

Usually, Sam watched out the side windows, but this morning something caught her eye at the front of the bus. That's when she happened to see the Blue Bird's beak tilt forward and drop from sight. In a matter of seconds, they were speeding downhill in a nose dive toward the Little River.

Up ahead, the rushing water churned the river's sandy bottom. Realizing they were headed straight for the water, she instinctively grabbed her life jacket and buckled it into place. After she pulled on her gloves, she reached for her hot pink canoe paddle.

Once she was suited up, she turned her attention back to the river, which was now so close that she

Laura Lea

could hear the hissing water as it fought to reach the reservoir.
We're moving too fast, she thought. *We'll take on too much water if we don't slow down!*
    The rains that had fallen over the last few days must have caused the river to swell, washing away the bridge. With panic overriding logic, she could think of no way to prevent the collision that was about to occur. There was only one thing left to do, prepare for the crash.
    Trying to remain calm, she wedged her right foot under the boom. Every muscle in her body tightened against the impact. The hissing sound she heard only moments earlier, was now an unmistakable roar.
    Before her, bubbling currents churned sand and gravel as if they were being pulsed together in some sort of Little River smoothie. Unable to sit still and just let this happen, she took hold of her hot pink paddle in a white-knuckled death grip, and began to back paddle.
    Unnhh, she growled, with each stroke.
    It was no use. Her efforts were having no effect on the raft's speed. Throwing her paddle to the floor, she wrapped her gloved hands around the guide ropes. Just before they hit the water, she took a deep breath and closed her eyes. From that moment on, everything happened in slow motion.
    SPLOUSH.
    All at once, cold, grainy water slapped her face, forcing her to come up for air. Every inch of her waterlogged body was covered with sludge from the river's bottom. She had slimy algae hanging from her left ear and last fall's decaying leaves clinging to her curls. With the hem of her wet tee-shirt, she tried to wipe away the dirt that now clung to her face. She

Cut from the Same Cloth

knew when she looked down at her shirt that she wasn't helping the situation at all. It, too, was covered with mud.

The moment she got to school she would make a beeline to the girl's restroom where she would attempt to clean her face. Hopefully, no one would even notice. After all, she did already have a gazillion freckles.

Before she realized where she was, her raft was floating up to the drop off point for the bus riders. Grabbing her backpack, she climbed out of the raft.

Hmm, she thought, *clear skies and sunshine. Bet I'll have to portage on my way back up stream.*

❋ ❂ ❋

*W*hen Miss Molly slid open the folding door, Sam adjusted her crown before stepping onto the red carpet. Blinded by the barrage of camera flashes, she held her pose, chin raised slightly to the left, pearly whites gleaming from ear to ear.

She stood still for what seemed like hours waiting for a lull in the activity. Finally, the flashes slowed. Squinting, she waited for her eyes to adjust. Then with all the grace of Miss America, she carefully descended the steps onto the crimson walkway.

She adored the attention, touching those who held their hands out to her. There was no time for autographs, she was already late. Continuing to make her way toward the front door, she was grateful the crowds pealed to let her pass. Suddenly, she heard the unmistakable sound of a bell ringing.

Laura Lea

"Oh, rats, I'm late for home room," Sam yelled, her crown falling to the floor as she sprinted through the door and down the hallway.

To Sam, school itself was her least favorite part of the school day. It was rather difficult to be famous during the whole bus ride to school only to find out that she was a big zero when she crossed the school's threshold. Unfortunately, she had never found a way to fit into any of the cliques in her grade.

When she was younger, the rejection bothered her, but over the last three years she had learned to accept it, even be okay with it.

Sam didn't mind being different. In fact, she rather liked it, especially since she knew it aggravated a certain group of girls in her class. They were tall, she was short. They wore dresses, she preferred jeans. They chose cute, trendy hair styles, she wore her golden curls, tied back in a bandanna or puddled on her shoulders. She had decided a long time ago that she was not willing to compromise just to be bumped up a few notches on the popularity poll. If they didn't want her, she didn't need them. Besides, she had Mickey Sullivan and he was all she needed.

On most days, Sam raced to get to the bus first so that she could stake her claim to the back seat. Anchored there, she would drop her backpack, plop herself down on the cracked, black vinyl bench, and pull her knees to her chest.

Once she was comfortable, she would unleash her mind. There were times when she was so focused on

Cut from the Same Cloth

her fantasies that she would lose track of where she was. Every time it happened, Sam would get frustrated with herself. So one day, she decided to memorize the bus route.

How hard could it be? she wondered. *After all, I travel these same roads two times a day, five days a week.*

So that's what she did.

In less than a week's time, she had memorized every bump and turn that the Blue Bird made between her house and school. She learned to recognize signs and brick colors, store front decorations and street numbers. Before long every business on Main Street was familiar. There had been several times when this load of seemingly insignificant knowledge had come in handy.

One day, Sam noticed that a little first grader was crying while riding the bus. She felt sorry for him, but Miss Molly had a list of bus rules, one of which was, *No Standing While The Bus Is In Motion*, and Sam had no intention of doing anything that might make her six foot tall bus driver angry.

Most of the time, she was a gentle giant, but every now and then, her temper would flare, causing her two gold, front teeth to appear, looking like flames shooting from the mouth of a dragon.

Dragon or no dragon, Sam thought, *C.J. needs me.*

Methodically, she planned her moves as though she was standing on a chess board. C.J. was only a short distance away, but she could not travel from her seat to his without breaking the rule. Taking her position, she became the rook. Her only options were to move horizontally and vertically, no diagonals allowed.

Keeping her eyes on the driver, she waited for Miss Molly to look down, then she moved forward two

Laura Lea

seats. Continuing to watch the front of the bus, she waited patiently for a chance to hop across the aisle.

"Hey, C.J., I'll be there in just a second," she yelled.

He turned to look at her, his tear stained cheeks begging her for help. Determined to reach him in one more move, the rook slid into the aisle, jumping vertically three rows ahead. Sliding in beside the crying boy, she threw her arm around his neck giving him her most sympathetic smile.

"Hey, what's wrong, C.J.?" she asked.

"I gotta go to the bathroom," the little boy cried.

"You gotta go to the bathroom. You've been crying all this time because you gotta go to the bathroom?"

"Uh-huh."

"Doesn't your mother work at the consignment shop on Main Street?"

"Uh-huh."

"It's just a few more blocks ahead. Look there, see that beige building on the corner up there?" Sam asked, pointing out the side window.

"Uh-huh."

"C.J., do you ever say anything besides 'uh-huh'?"

"Uh-huh."

"Ooooh," Sam groaned. "Hey, look, isn't that your mom standing by the curb?"

"Yeah," C.J. sang.

"C.J., come on down," boomed Miss Molly.

"Bye, Sam. Thanks," smiled C.J.

With that, he headed toward the front of the bus, bounded down the steps, and ran as fast as his legs would carry him through the front door of Repeats, the local consignment shop with his mom chasing after him.

Sam was glad that she had been able to put her route knowledge to good use. A tiring day at school

Cut from the Same Cloth

behind her, Sam made her way to the back bench. In no mood to chat, she dropped her pack on the floor and leaned her head against the mud splattered window, willing her mind's eye to focus.

Moments later, a colorful array of shops and businesses were clearly visible somewhere in her head. There was quite an assortment of sizes and colors standing shoulder to shoulder, as if they were guarding the eternal flame that burned continually in the center of the town square.

On the corner to the right side of the bus stood a sturdy brown brick building with beige trim and black shutters. Sam didn't have to open her eyes to identify the business. It was the only law office in Providence, and it belonged to Bill and Sue Dailey. Though Sam had never been inside, it looked like a snooty place.

A few doors down on the same side of the street was Sawyer Wood's hardware store. There was no way that Sam could pass by the hardware store without sneaking a peek. For as long as she could remember, there had been a real toilet sitting front and center behind the store's large, green-tinted, plate glass window. Propped on the back of the toilet was an old handwritten sign that read, "Don't flush your money down the toilet. Shop with us."

On the corner, by the town's only traffic light stood the Breakfast in Bed Café. Recognizing it was never very hard for Sam even with her eyes closed. If she was lucky, Miss Molly would have to stop for the red light and the smell of freshly baked muffins would fill the bus.

Uurrhh. The bus rolled to a stop.

"This must be my lucky day," she whispered, thinking aloud.

Laura Lea

Breathing deeply, the sweet smell of cinnamon filled her nostrils before heading to her lungs. Her mouth began to water. She licked her lips hoping to find even the tiniest morsel of sugar remaining from the candy she had shared with her friend, Mickey, during lunch.

The Breakfast in Bed Café was Sam and Gommy's favorite restaurant. The owners, Harold and Marcie had done a great job converting the old Tuggle's Menswear building into the best restaurant and bakery in the county.

The smell of cinnamon reminded her of sticky buns, and sticky buns reminded her of Gommy. A flutter of anticipation grabbed her heart. She sat up in her seat, the map quest over, and wondered how her grandmother was doing. Gommy had been in the hospital for nearly a week and Sam was ready for her to come home.

I wonder if Mom's back from the hospital yet, she thought. *Maybe she even brought Gommy home.*

Surely, it wouldn't be much longer. Just thinking about her grandmother spending so much time alone in the hospital made Sam's heart hurt. She didn't want to think about the hospital or about the pneumonia that put her grandmother there to start with.

Chuusshh.

Jerking her slightly, the bus lurched forward just as Sam turned to see the white lace curtains of the café slowly disappear. Craning her neck, she tried to see out the front window. From the traffic light, it would take about ten minutes to reach her road.

Just beyond the town square, the landscape began to change. Gravel replaced concrete and, rather than brick buildings, tall oaks and pines clustered beside

Cut from the Same Cloth

the roadways. In town, adults and children roamed the streets and sidewalks. In the rural areas, cows and goats were constantly looking for greener pastures.

Sam watched as Miss Molly used her whole body to turn the steering wheel. As far as Sam could see, Copper Hill Road slithered along side the upper fence that ran the length of her mother's property like a snake in search of its next meal.

Sam had lived her entire life on Copper Hill Road. Perfectly named, it was home to acres and acres of tall pasture grass that spent the early fall and winter months dressed in golden spires tipped with crimson seeds. Sometimes as the sun was ending its day, a golden glow would settle on the pasture, making it look as though a raging fire had burned the land leaving behind a field of glowing embers.

Anxious to get home so that she could check on her grandmother, Sam really wished Miss Molly would put 'the pedal to the metal' just this once, even if it meant they'd be taking their chances as they passed over the mine field of holes left by the recent torrential rains. Laying her head against the back of the seat, her mind began to wander.

In a matter of seconds, she was in another world. There, she found herself planted on the rear crest of a giant bug's slimy tongue. Samantha Louise Parker peered through the slits that were its eyes, wondering how she got in this predicament in the first place. She and her fellow prisoners were being held captive by a villain they had yet to identify.

As the bus rolled to a halt, Sam was thrown toward its massive opening.

Shhhhhhhhh, screeeeee.

The sound of its mighty jaws shook her to action as the driver opened the sliding door. Sam knew she

Laura Lea

must act now or another victim would soon become its prey. She alone would have to slay the ugly beast. The others were far too frightened to help. Only Sam had the courage to save them.

Grabbing a pencil from her backpack, she now held a glistening, golden dagger, and with it she must cast a deadly blow. There would only be one chance to inflict a mortal wound. She could not fail.

Holding the dagger before her, she took aim. Her target was the monster's slimy jaw. With all of her strength, she hurled the dagger.

It seemed to move in slow motion as it sliced through the air. There was complete silence as the other prisoners held their breath waiting for the dagger to strike the grotesque gums of the giant. Reaching its target, the dagger disappeared, lodging deeply in the jaw of their captor. The giant groaned, spilling drool as it thrashed its massive head.

Samantha felt sure she would die, as the lurching larvae tossed her onto the floor. After what seemed like hours, the spiny giant ceased its motion. When Samantha realized she had defeated her captor, she dragged herself up, wiping its slimy drool from her clothes.

That is when she first heard the sound. It was faint, unrecognizable. Gradually, it grew into a low rumble. The chanting continued, growing into a deafening roar. It was then that Samantha understood the words.

"Hail, Samantha. Long live, Samantha," they chanted. Knowing her pride was justified, she gathered her belongings and bowed to her comrades. Only she had found the courage to slay the beast, and singlehandedly, she had done just that.

Cut from the Same Cloth

As she gallantly made her way to freedom, she was momentarily blinded by the brightest light she had seen in days. Raising her hand to shield her eyes from the intense light, she was forced to squint while she waited for her sight to return. When the dark spots in her vision faded, she confirmed what her legs and feet had already told her.

"Ooh, gross," she sighed, noticing her feet were submerged in a huge, mud puddle. The cold, muddy sludge crawled slowly down her legs, bringing her back to reality. The game was over.

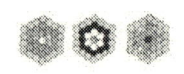

❋ ❂ ❋

Turning toward the driver, she yelled, "Thanks, Miss Molly, see ya tomorrow."

"Samantha Louise Parker, you be careful on that driveway, ya hear?" Miss Molly yelled. "Oh, and, how's Gommy, hon?"

"Alright, I guess. Mom was going to see her this morning. Maybe she got to bring Gommy home with her."

"I shore hope so, hon. I know you miss her somethin' fierce. Well, tell ya momma I said hey, and I hope Gommy gets to come home real soon."

"I will," Sam yelled, over the idling bus engine. She turned and squished her way toward her house, backpack and all.

Sam really liked Miss Molly. It had taken a week or two to get to know her, but the two of them had been friends ever since. The only complaint Sam had about Molly was that she insisted on calling her by her entire name, Samantha Louise Parker. No one else ever

Laura Lea

called her Samantha Louise, not even her own mother. Most people called her Sam, and that's the way she liked it.

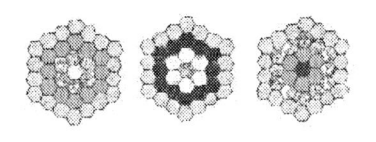

Chapter 4
The Arrival of Spring

Scanning the horizon, Sam saw her mother's van parked under the carport. As she ran toward the house, her golden curls flew about her face licking the tiny drops of sweat as quickly as they appeared on her forehead. Glancing skyward, she scowled at the one responsible for her erratic movements. Most days, she felt steady on her feet, but today was a different story. Today she felt quite helpless, dangling from her puppeteer's hands. Why was it necessary to have her slip and slide on the loose gravel?

Hey, what's going on up there? she wondered.

Unwilling to spend another second dangling out of control, she jerked her hands and feet as hard as she could, breaking the strings that held her to the dancing, wooden crosses controlling her from above. Finally, she was free to move under her own power.

Slowing her pace to a trot, Sam let her eyes feast on the arrival of spring. Everything around her seemed clean and bright. Amazed at how quickly the

Cut from the Same Cloth

weather could change, she marveled at the transformation she was now seeing. Earlier in the week, a freak, spring snow had fallen while the town slept, leaving behind a fluffy white blanket that covered the entire countryside.

Sam remembered being awakened by the glaring light that poured in through her bedroom window. Leaping from the foot of her bed to the window in a single bound, she mashed her forehead and nose against the chilly glass pane.

Amazed at the panoramic view before her, Sam couldn't believe her eyes. Even in the dead of winter, Providence rarely got more than a dusting of snow, so waking to find three inches in early April was truly a welcome surprise. The pear-shaped cloud of moisture her breath left on the cool glass convinced her that she wasn't dreaming.

All around her house, pristine pastures were quietly waiting for the first touch of life. The morning was still and quiet. Tempted to grab her slippers and head for the yard, Sam wondered who or what would be first to leave its impression on the unmarked snow.

By the following day, the temperatures had risen above freezing, and all that remained was a fine dusting of dirt on everything that was once covered with snow. Since then, a band of storms had blown through, washing everything clean.

Thinking the pasture might still be soggy, Sam decided to trot along the gravel drive even though its sweeping curves would make her trip a good bit longer. She was surprised to find the ground almost dry. It had been a dirty sponge soaking up the water almost as quickly as it fell. The only exception was the muddy water still cradled by the deep pot holes that dotted the drive.

Laura Lea

Living on a hill, breezes were an everyday occurrence. Even now as Sam neared her house, she could feel the gentle wind drying the beads of sweat from her face and arms. All around her, the tall grass swayed, bowing to her as she passed.

Today was a glorious day, and she had no intention of spending a single minute of it cooped up in the house. The rainy weather that moved into Providence nearly a month ago, appeared to be ready to move on. Finally, free to revel in being outside again, today's warm air and sunshine felt incredible on her skin.

The closer she got to the house the more excited she became. Up ahead, the ladder-like rungs of the monkey bars were waiting. Maybe she would even play King of the Mountain and stand on the top just once. Huffing and puffing, she climbed the hill wondering if she should lighten her load by dropping her backpack. She could always go back for it later.

"Come on, you can make it, it's not far now," Sam told herself. With her heart pounding and her lungs begging for more air, she made her final approach, dodging the remaining potholes.

By the time, she reached her mother's dusty mini van, she feared her chest might pop. Propping her backside against the rear bumper, she bent over, resting her hands on her knees for support. With her head dangling between her legs, she tried to spell her name on the concrete with the drops of sweat that rolled off her chin. When the task was complete, she raised her head slowly to keep from becoming lightheaded.

Annoyed by the sweat that still poured from her brow, she yanked on her shirt, untucking it from her

Cut from the Same Cloth

pants. Anxious to dry her face, she made several swipes with the hem of her shirt.

Ooh, disgusting, she thought, as she spied the heavy film of dirt and moisture that now covered the wadded corner of her shirt.

Even though she was pooped from the trek up the drive, there was something energizing about the clear, blue sky that hung above her. All at once, she felt fit for her next adventure.

❊ ✪ ❊

Sam lived with her mother, Jillian Parker, and her grandmother, Louise Black. At 5'3, Jillian was short and very thin. Her chin length, light brown curls framed her freckled face, showcasing her china blue eyes.

Appearing older than her thirty-seven years, her face wore the tiny wrinkles gained from spending countless hours in the sun without the protection of sunscreen. An attractive woman, she rarely smiled, usually appearing overly serious. On those rare occasions when she did relax and smile, she could have been Sam's older sister. The resemblance was uncanny.

When Sam was a baby, and just learning to talk, she found it difficult to pronounce the word 'grandmother'. At first, she tried to say "gand mommy" but Gommy was as close as she could get. So Gommy it was. The new name caught on quickly, and before long the entire town was calling Louise Black by her new name.

Laura Lea

A few years ago, Sam's mom and grandmother bought her a play set. The moment Sam saw it, she was in love. The monstrous green and yellow structure held the usual items; swings, monkey bars, a slide, and a rock wall, but the clubhouse perched above the slide quickly became Sam's special hideaway.

The tree house, as she called it, had become her sanctuary. Gommy, on the other hand, called it her Pity Palace. Sam could go there to sort out her emotions in private, never having to worry about unwanted company.

The most awesome thing about her five foot square hideaway was that it was the perfect friend. It was always there waiting for her. Within its four walls, she could bare her soul with no worry that her confidence would be betrayed. Over the years, Sam had learned to be grateful that stuffed bears and wooden walls could not speak.

❋ ✪ ❋

*H*er heart calm, and her breathing steady, she lunged for the back door to the house, slung it open, and threw her book bag onto the floor.

"Mooom, I'm hooome," she sang, "How's Gommy?"

"Hey, Sam," her mom called as she entered the kitchen carrying a stack of dish towels. "I need to talk to you abo—."

Before she could finish her sentence, the back door slammed shut, and Sam made a mad dash for the swing. Pulling the white lace curtains to the side

Cut from the Same Cloth

of the kitchen window, Jillian Parker watched as her daughter hopped onto the swing and began to pump her short legs wildly.

Jillian enjoyed watching Sam play from her kitchen window. This allowed her to keep an eye on her daughter while she did her housework.

There was a time when she didn't think they should spend the money on the play set, but Gommy had insisted, saying she would buy it herself if Jillian didn't want to split the cost. Trying to talk her mother out of the purchase would have been useless–Gommy could be quite stubborn–so buy it they did.

About a week before Christmas, a group of men from the First Methodist Church came by at Gommy's pleading and put the set together while Sam was away at school.

"Mom, Mom," Sam yelled as she ran up the drive that afternoon. "What's that? Whose is it? Whose, Mom? Tell me, tell me."

"I got it for Gommy." Jillian yelled, trying not to laugh. "It's her Christmas gift."

Even before Sam reached the play set, her mood change was evident. It had taken her approximately three seconds to plummet from joyful anticipation to utter despair.

"Why the look?" Jillian called. "Oh, all right. It's for you, Sam. Merry Christmas."

With only a few yards between Sam and the gigantic green and gold play set, she reached it in no time at all. Grinning ear to ear, she climbed the ladder that led to the monkey bars. Balancing on the top rung, she reached forward to grab the first rung.

In a matter of seconds, her dusty, pink sneakers were dangling at the far end of the play set. Laughing

Laura Lea

uncontrollably, she spun around and quickly made her return trip.

It would be difficult to forget the look on Sam's face as she dropped to the ground. She was both proud and awestruck, momentarily speechless. Her mother had never known her to smile so broadly. Jillian wondered if it was possible to show every tooth in a single smile. Maybe, maybe not, but on this particular day, Sam made it look delightfully easy.

Since that day, Sam made it a point to spend every possible minute outside. Through sheer determination and a lot of practice, she mastered every part of the play set except for the swing. She couldn't really understand why she had a mental block about the whole swing thing. It was so out of character. Ordinarily, she was the 'no fear' kid.

Today would be the day she would conquer the silly, old swing. The perfect weather was all the encouragement she needed. Today, she was going to force herself to jump from the flying swing.

Pumping the swing, her muscled legs propelled her higher. The monotonous motion freed her mind to revisit Providence Primary School, and all that had happened there today.

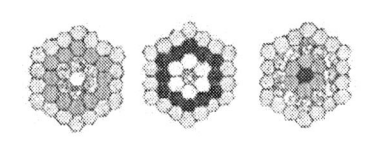

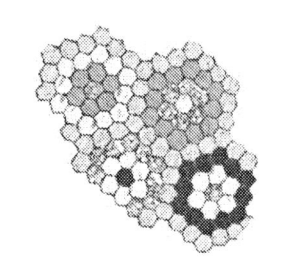

Chapter 5
Mickey Sullivan

Once again, her mother had forgotten to pack her lunch, forcing her to make a selection from the school cafeteria line. Not caring for a Salisbury Steak, she opted for the kid-friendly choice, a sloppy Joe sandwich, French fries, a moon pie, and the vegetable of the millennium, 'slima beans'.

Sam couldn't understand why the ladies in the cafeteria felt compelled to serve those pasty, little balls of green yuck every other day. As far as she could remember, she had never seen a single kid eat the first bean. Was it possible that the cafeteria cooks had never heard *The Rhyme*?

"Beans, beans, make you smart," Sam thought smiling to herself.

Somewhat of a loner, Sam preferred the single friend approach. For as long as she could remember, her single friend had been Mickey Sullivan. With Mickey for a pal, she didn't have much need for anyone else.

Cut from the Same Cloth

He was not only smart, but he was dependable. A nine-year-old with reddish-orange freckles and hair so short that it looked like his bald head had been dusted with ground cinnamon, Mickey was adorably cute.

Standing side by side, they were definitely a pair. Both shorter than the average nine-year-old and covered with freckles, they were hard to miss even in a crowd. They met in the first grade and had been best friends ever since.

Sometimes their teacher, Miss Allen, would try to pair them up with other kids in the class, but it never lasted. They were like two magnets with opposing poles. Eventually, they would find each other again.

One of the things Sam liked most about Mickey was that he wasn't like the other boys in her grade. Somehow, he had outgrown being gross early. She couldn't remember him ever trying to make bathroom noises with his underarm, and he never told disgusting jokes.

In Sam's mind, it was his generosity that made him special. He was always offering her part of his lunch, especially since her mother had been on a health kick.

On the days when her mother remembered to pack a lunch for her, it was filled with healthy stuff, like little midget carrots and tuna salad on wheat.

Yuck.

Most nine-year-olds wouldn't be caught dead eating midget carrots in front of their friends, and tuna salad on wheat.... What was her mother thinking? Just the smell of it would make her the brunt of all the jokes.

Now Mickey's mom, on the other hand, knew how to pack a killer lunch. Usually his bag contained

Laura Lea

a veritable smorgasbord of great foods like push-up yogurt, cheese doodles, and fruit chews. Thankfully, his mother knew that he frequently shared his lunch, so she would include doubles on the doodles and chews.

❈ ✪ ❈

One afternoon, while Sam and her mother were getting dinner on the table, they started talking about school. As it often did, the conversation drifted to Mickey. Sam didn't usually confide in her mother, preferring instead to talk to her grandmother. This time, however, she had no choice. With Gommy in the hospital, her mother was her only option. At first, she was a little uncomfortable, unsure of what to expect, but before she knew it her problem was out in the open.

"Mom, the girls in my class keep teasing me. They keep singing this stupid, old song, about me and Mickey."

Standing perfectly still, both hands on her hips, she began to sing the words in a mocking tone, "Sam and Mickey sittin' in a tree, k-i-s-s-i-n-g. First comes love—."

Sam stopped suddenly at the sound of her mother's voice singing along.

"...i-n-g. First comes loves, then comes marriage, then comes Sam with a ba—." Jillian stopped in mid sentence.

"Mom," Sam sighed with disgust, "not you, too. It's bad enough that I have to hear it at school, do I have to hear it at home, too?"

Cut from the Same Cloth

"I know, you're right, it's just that I remember that little rhyme from when I was in grammar school. We used to sing it all the time. Boy, Sam, that's an old one. I can't believe it's still around."

"I don't sing it!" Sam barked. "I'm the one they sing it about. It's embarrassing." Sam watched for her mother's reaction, but all she got was a huge smile.

"Mom, it's not funny. I can't stand it. It makes Mickey boiling mad, too."

"Sam, you can't let other kids get to you like that. They probably don't mean to hurt your feelings. Anyway, you have to admit, you and Mickey do spend a whole lot of time together. You know, the girls are probably just jealous. Let me guess, is one of these girls Mary Sue Ingersoll?"

"Yeah."

"Well, there you have it. The two of you have been battling for Mickey's attention since the first grade. She's jealous, that's all it is. Best if you just ignore her and her buddies."

"But, Mom, that's kinda hard to do. She's got such a big mouth and all. You know she's really loud."

"Well, Sam, you may as well learn to ignore people like Mary Sue, 'cause they're always gonna be out there."

Sam thought for a moment about her mother's sage advise. For the first time in her life, she actually thought her mother might be trying to be helpful. Wanting to keep the conversation going, Sam brought up the next dilemma.

"Mom," she said, her brow wrinkled. "Is Mickey my boyfriend? Or is he just a *boy* friend?" Sam asked, both confused and embarrassed.

"Hmm, where did that come from? I never expected to hear you ask a question like that. You're a

Laura Lea

little young to be wondering about something like that, don't you think? You're only nine years old."

"Mom, this is serious."

"Well, you're too young to have a *boyfriend*, so I guess that would technically make Mickey a friend who just happens to be a boy. So that's all you have to call him. You know, just leave the word *boy* out of it. Everybody already knows he's a boy, so there's really no point in even bringing it up."

"Mom," Sam hesitated, "when I turn ten years old can Mickey be my boyfriend?"

The heel of her palm against her forehead, Jillian was at a loss. "Why don't we wait 'til then to discuss this?"

She couldn't help but realize that her daughter was growing up, and she really didn't know her very well. Maybe she had not handled Sam's problem very well, but she was sure her daughter had gotten the message. The subject of boyfriends was temporarily off limits.

Maybe Sam was to blame for the situation with the girls in her class. She had never really tried too make friends with any of them. It required far to much energy to look past the whole prissy, cutesy thing with all of their ribbons and lace. They were absolutely far too prissy for her taste.

She knew they thought she was a tomboy. There were times when she could see it written on their faces and hear it from their lips. Mockery was a game they played at her expense. There was no love lost between them, and after years of being the brunt of their snide comments, she tried not to let it bother her. After all, she didn't really need them anyway, she had Mickey.

Cut from the Same Cloth

Sam thought about Mickey a lot. She was constantly discovering things they had in common, one of which was he loved the beach, and she was sure that, if she ever got to go there, she would love it too.

When Mickey was four years old, his parents divorced and his dad moved to the beach. Every year since then, Mickey and his sister, Darla, would visit their dad during the summer break. For eight weeks, he got to play on the beach and swim in the ocean.

Sam had seen some of his pictures, and it had been exactly like she thought it would be. Once, he even brought her a conch shell so that she could hear the sound of the waves crashing on the shore.

Another thing they had in common was their December birthdays. Sam couldn't stand having a birthday during the month of Christmas. Most of the time, people were too busy to put much thought into her gift. Every year her presents would come wrapped in holiday paper. Talk about the pits.

Sam and Mickey loved to run and were both really fast, especially Mickey. As far as Sam could remember, he had never lost a race to her or anyone else. Mickey was by far the fastest guy in her class, maybe even in her whole school.

She loved thinking about Mickey, but for the moment, she thought it best if she concentrated her attention on the business at hand.

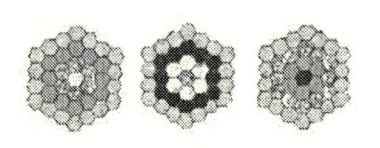

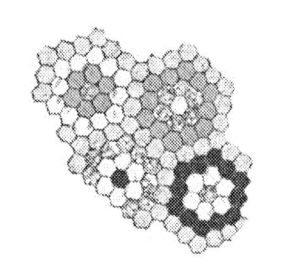

Chapter 6
Chicken Poop & Sweet Corn

The sun was a fiery magnet drawing her closer as she swung higher and higher. It had been so long since she had seen the sun, her skin soaked it in greedily, letting it warm her all over. Amazingly, she was both warm and cool at the same time. It was one of the wondrous contradictions that went with living on a hill in the middle of a pasture. There was nothing quite like the feeling of being kissed by a refreshing breeze on a warm day. Sometimes, her skin would pop with excitement, leaving behind a temporary covering of chill bumps.

With all of the rain, it had been nearly a week since she had gotten to play outside. Glad for the nice weather, she laughed as the swing took her higher. Golden ringlets tickled her nose as they flew freely about her head. Her senses were enjoying the birth of spring. There was so much to take in, so much to see again for the first time. Waking from its long winter nap, the world around her eagerly stretched, reaching

Cut from the Same Cloth

for the sun. Everywhere she looked, fresh shades of lime green could be seen peeking from under their earthen blankets.

As her eyes feasted on all that lay before her, she was fascinated by the mix of smells that floated on the breeze. Today, the gentle breeze carried with it a seasonal guest.

It was impossible for her to mistake the odor that filled the air around her. It was the smell of chicken poop being mixed into the freshly tilled soil. Mr. Bill, her neighbor, was busy preparing the ground for his annual corn crop. Each spring he would carefully till composted chicken manure into his garden. He was positive this was the secret to his successful crop each year. Sam was a bit skeptical of the whole chicken poop thing, but she had to agree with Mr. Bill, he did grow the sweetest corn in the entire county.

Raising her hand, she waved wildly at her favorite neighbor. Normally, he would have removed his red cowboy hat and waved it in her direction, but today his mind was on his pasture. Planting day was just around the corner, leaving no time for a joy ride.

Just the sight of him made her smile. Burned into her memory was the image of Mr. Bill wearing his faded red cowboy hat, bouncing around on his old, rusty, gray tractor.

Sam thought Miss Edna, his wife, was probably right about his appearance. She had said, on more than one occasion, that he looked like a worn out, old cowboy riding a worn out, old mule, and he moved about half as fast. It was no secret that she thought the old tractor should be put out to pasture, but his response was always the same when Miss Edna started fussing about his tractor.

"Don't recalls asking you, Edna," he would say.

Laura Lea

It was easy to tell when it was plowing time, Miss Edna would become more cranky than normal. Mr. Bill didn't seem to mind though, he'd just keep plugging along until he got the job done. Sam knew that as far as her favorite farmer was concerned, there was nothing better than a sunny day spent riding his old tractor, Bessie.

※ ✪ ※

As Sam continued to swing, she decided this was the perfect day to make the long-anticipated leap from the soaring swing. Until now, she had been too chicken to try. Today, however, she felt brave, even a little daring. After all, if she could defeat a giant monster all by herself, surely she could jump from a flying swing.
Piece of cake, she thought. *It's now or never.*
Gathering her courage, she began to swing herself higher and higher, waiting for the perfect moment to leap from the swing.
Come on, Sam. You can do this, she chided. *How hard can it be? If Mickey can do it, so can you.*
Everytime she felt the urge to jump, though, her white-knuckled death grip on the swing's chains prevented her from letting go.
Maybe another approach would do the trick. She could count down like they do at the Space Center. After swearing on a stack of Gommy's Bibles, she promised herself that she would jump when she reached zero, NO MATTER WHAT, and thus, her countdown began.

Cut from the Same Cloth

"Ten, nine, eight, seven, six, five, four—," she yelled.

Afraid she might lose her nerve, she abandoned the count. Flying gracefully from the swing, she was a beautiful lady, hurtling head long from the bowels of a glossy, black circus cannon.

Wiping down the sink in front of the window, Sam's mother watched as her daughter flew through the air. Momentarily stunned, she gasped, then quickly looked away, unable to watch for fear that her daredevil daughter might land wrong and break a bone. Waiting several seconds, she slowly turned back towards the window expecting to see her daughter crying in a heap on the pea gravel beneath the play set. Surprisingly, Sam had survived the landing and was now running around, waving her arms wildly, grinning ear to ear, obviously proud of her accomplishment.

Exhaling deeply, Jillian realized she had been holding her breath. Thankful for her daughter's safe landing, she quickly raised the kitchen window and yelled her congratulations.

"Hey, Sam, that was beautiful. But you better be careful!"

"Hey, Mom," Sam yelled back, "I did it, Mom, I did it. I finally jumped. Yea. Wanna see me do it again?"

"Please, be careful, Sam," Jillian called to her daughter. "And I really need for you to come in soon. We need to talk."

Surprised to see Sam finally make the big jump, she knew exactly what to expect. Seconds later, a mass of arms and legs were crawling across the top of the monkey bars.

Leaving the window open in case her daughter called for help, Jillian could hear old Bessie as she

Laura Lea

rattled her way up and down the rows of Mr. Bill's garden. Scanning the pasture, she could see the rows of freshly tilled soil chasing Mr. Bill and his tractor.

Jillian loved the springtime. It was the time of year when everything around her seemed excited to be alive, but this year enjoying it had been especially difficult. With Gommy in the hospital, nothing seemed normal.

Taking a deep breath, she hoped to smell the earthy scent of Mr. Bill's freshly turned soil.

"Ooh," she said aloud, wincing at the pungent odor. "Chicken poop again?"

Today, it would be impossible to smell the rich, black earth. Instead, she would be forced to endure the foul odor as it announced the arrival of spring.

Wrinkling her nose as she took another whiff, she couldn't believe it was that time of year already. Had she been so preoccupied with her mother's illness that she had somehow missed an entire month? It couldn't be Easter already. Glancing at the little Flower of the Month calendar that sat on the kitchen window sill, her suspicion was confirmed. It was that time again. The disgusting odor floating through her kitchen window was definitely that of chicken poop. Her neighbor was at it again.

During the ten years that Jillian had lived next door to Mr. Bill, she couldn't remember him ever missing a planting day. According to all of the local farmers, Good Friday was the best day to put the seeds in the ground. Getting a reasonable explanation as to why this was the case had been practically impossible. Even Mr. Bill didn't know why he did it that way. "It's just the way we do it," he had told her when she pressed him for an answer. After asking

Cut from the Same Cloth

around, the general consensus was that it had more to do with tradition than anything else.

Mr. Bill had been a serious farmer since he retired from the Hamden County school system eighteen years ago. He didn't depend on his crops for income, just for entertainment. In the early years, he took great pains to experiment with different types of fertilizer and watering techniques, hoping to find the perfect combination of the two.

Finally, after about seven years of serious effort, he hit the jackpot. Just the right mix of chicken poop and water proved to be the winning combination. When word of his success fanned out around the county, several of the local farmers begged him to divulge his secret. Of course, it didn't take long for the word to get out, considering that it's fairly difficult to disguise the smell of chicken poop.

Soon, the whole town was talking about it. Unfortunately, Mr. Bill became the butt of many farming jokes. Unaffected by their humor, Mr. Bill was adamant about his chicken poop formula, insisting that manure was the key to his successful corn crop each year.

"Jillian," Mr. Bill had said, "I know you think I'm just a crazy, old coot, but it's tried and true, works ever' time."

Apparently, he was right. Folks came from all over the county to buy corn from Mr. Bill. His corn was the best, winning the blue ribbon at the county fair for nine of the past eleven years.

Hailed the undisputed *King of Corn*–a title he accepted with great honor–Mr. Bill became a local celebrity. Everywhere he went, people would bow or curtsy to him. Miss Edna, however, didn't like it one bit.

Laura Lea

"Bill," she would say, "don't you know all them folks are makin' fun of you? They're probably laughin' at the both of us b'hind our backs." If they were, it didn't bother him one bit. He would just smile and tip his worn-out red cowboy hat when the jesting began.

❁ ✿ ❁

Continuing to scrub the white porcelain sink, Jillian caught a glimpse of Sam crouched on the top of the monkey bars prowling across its rungs like a cat.

Oh, Sam, why can't you be like everyone else and just hang from the bars? Jillian thought. There was never a moment's rest when it came to worrying about Sam.

What is it that makes you crave being different? she wondered.

Her daughter was fearless. Why did that surprise her? Sam's father had been the same way. Jillian couldn't help but smile. Sam was just like him.

It's her courage, she thought. *That's what reminds me so of Peter.*

Eyes trained on her daughter, it was possible to see the definition of her flexed muscles as she climbed with ease over the play set. She looked amazingly strong for someone her size.

After a few minutes spent watching her daughter, Jillian realized that the young lady playing out in the yard was a stranger. Even though, her eyes told her she was watching her daughter, the figure before her seemed all grown up, not really very much like the little girl she always pictured in her mind when she thought of her only child.

Cut from the Same Cloth

Why does it feel like you're someone else's child? I feel so far away from you, Jillian thought.

For the past week, Jillian had been putting a lot of thought into the relationship she had with her daughter. With Gommy in the hospital, there was no one there to be the sounding board, no one to bridge the gap between mother and daughter. It had not been terrible, just a little strained. Jillian and Sam had been courteous to each other, yet there was little attempt by either one to take the relationship deeper. For the first time, the distance seemed unnatural and started Jillian to wondering.

All week she had been struggling to put her finger on the problem that was so clearly present in their relationship. It had been a time of observation and soul searching. Until today, she had been unable to pin point anything specific. Yet now, as she studied the young lady who was busy conquering the world, the answer seemed as clear as the window pane through which she was gazing.

The two of them were strangers. There was no need to waste another minute wondering who was to blame or how it actually happened. The answer was obvious. Jillian knew she was to blame. During Sam's first two years, her care had been all consuming. Yet the day her father died, everything changed.

First, there were the years spent trying to come to terms with her husband's death. Once Jillian was able to accept that he was not coming back, the decision to return to school became her priority. Her grueling course schedule kept her away from home both night and day. Eventually, she finished school and began the time-consuming task of building her business. And that's where she was now. Jillian had become a relatively successful event planner. It had never been

Laura Lea

her intention to ignore her child, but that is exactly what happened. Now she and Sam were *strangers*.

Ashamed of herself for allowing the situation to become this serious, Jillian realized that she didn't know her daughter well enough to lead her through the darkness that was ahead. In a matter of minutes she was going to rip her daughter's safety net right out from under her, leaving her alone with no one she trusted to catch her when she fell. Jillian knew she would be Sam's only hope, but was she up to the task?

Mother and daughter were about to head out into uncharted waters. Jillian, taking on the responsibility of caring for her daughter, and Sam allowing her do it. Right now, she would give her right arm for just a smidgen of her daughter's courage.

"Oh, Sam," she sighed closing her eyes as if she could wish the whole thing away. "How on earth am I gonna tell you about Mom?"

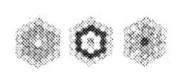

❀ ✪ ❀

*A*ware that her mother was watching her from the kitchen window, Sam carefully crossed the draw bridge that covered the fiery moat. Once she reached the edge of the wooden plank, she leaped as far as her short legs would carry her. Landing on her head, she did the old tuck and roll maneuver, hoping to keep her armor intact. Rolling herself into the standing position, she threw her arms straight into the air, arched her back, and raised her chin, the perfect gymnast.

Cut from the Same Cloth

    Surrounded by a sea of peasants, she could hear their voices rumbling around her, their eyes wide at the sight of their new queen. With her heart still pounding and the sensation that she might have caught her clothing on fire as she crossed the moat, she turned quickly looking over her left shoulder. To her surprise, the draw bridge had been consumed by fire and was now gone, swallowed up by the flaming moat.
    At that instant, she realized the reason for the heat. With the draw bridge no longer in place, she was teetering on the rim of the moat, dangerously close to the raging flames. Just as she started to lunge away from the flames, a masked man with red hair appeared from out of nowhere. Swinging past, he reached his sweat-drenched arm around her waist and carried her to safety.
    As she lay on the ground, a safe distance from the flames, the crowd of onlookers exploded with applause. This time it was not meant for her, but rather for the red-haired stranger, who was now nowhere to be found.
    Their words rained down on her, cooling the heat that had just moments ago threatened her life. Her subjects were grateful for the courage she showed in freeing them from the giant monster. Their voices were also raised to honor the stranger who saved their new queen.
    While waving regally to her subjects, she watched the dispersing crowd hoping to catch another glimpse of her hero. She had been unable to thank him or even ask his name. Disappointed in the turn of events, she noticed that her hero had dropped his scarf. Stooping gracefully to pick up the crimson

Laura Lea

cloth, she noticed initials embroidered in royal blue, M.S.

Ah-ha, it was just as she had suspected. Sir Michael Sullivan had come to her rescue, yet again.

She wanted desperately to run and find Sir Michael, but she knew that her people needed her to protect them, care for them, even advise them. She was no stranger to their plight. At that moment, she knew she would risk everything to protect them, even if it meant she might never see Sir Michael again.

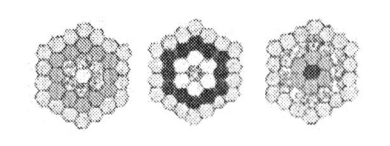

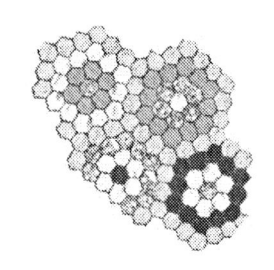

Chapter 7
The Reason for the Rift

From the kitchen window, Sam's curls could be seen blowing in the breeze. With the afternoon sun glinting their tips, a golden halo glistened around her moist, pink face crowning her the new queen.

Knowing she couldn't delay any longer, Jillian opened the porch door and called to her daughter.

"Hey, Sam, come on in. I need to talk to you."

"Oh, Mom, I just got out here. Can't I stay just a little longer? I haven't gotten to play outside in a long time."

"Not now, honey. Come—."

"But, Mom,—." Sam interrupted.

Jillian knew she needed to get this over with, but maybe Sam was right. Because of the heavy spring rains, her daughter had been stuck in the house for days. Just a little while longer couldn't hurt. Besides, Jillian was definitely not in a hurry to break the news to Sam. As she approached the window to let Sam know she could stay out a little longer, she saw her

Cut from the Same Cloth

daughter scoot down the ladder and make her way toward the house.

"I'm coming," Sam yelled as though she knew she had no choice.

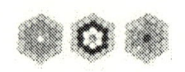

❖ ◎ ❖

*J*illian finished putting away the dish towels and started scrubbing the cabinets and counters.

Oh, Mom, she thought, *I wish you were here. Sam needs you. I need you!*

Jillian couldn't decide how much Sam should be told about her grandmother's condition. Ordinarily, it was her habit to be totally honest with Sam except when the topic was Peter. Otherwise, honesty had always served her well. It really was the best policy. This time, however, she just wasn't sure.

Did Sam really need to know all of the details? Her head told her to tell Sam the truth. *She's tough. She can handle it.* But her heart wanted to shield her daughter from the sadness that was just over their horizon.

Death was never easy. Jillian knew this first hand. So, this time she would make an exception. For Sam's sake, as well as her own, she let her heart win. She would spare her daughter as long as she could.

Jillian knew Sam well enough to know that if Gommy died, she would be heartbroken. Sam was very close to her grandmother. As far as Jillian was concerned, her mother and her daughter were best friends.

In the beginning, Jillian resented their closeness. Theirs was a bond that she and her mother never enjoyed. A little jealous, at first, she eventually

Laura Lea

accepted their relationship, learning to be happy for the two of them.

She was thrilled that the two girls in her life were getting along so well, yet, she was also confused. Who was this woman that she had called Mom for thirty-seven years? The person, lovingly caring for her daughter, was not the same woman that barely had any time for her when she was a child. Something had changed. Jillian didn't really know what it was, but she was glad that it had for Sam's sake.

For the most part, the situation had worked out well for the three of them. Jillian had started her catering business, Sam had been showered with attention, and Gommy had found great fulfillment in her retirement years.

The only problem was that somewhere along the way, Sam began to think of her grandmother as her mother, and her mother became a visitor in their home. At first, it was subtle, but as the years passed, it became quite clear to Jillian that her daughter didn't need her at all. Definitely grateful for her mother's help and the freedom it provided, she knew that it had cost her her relationship with her daughter.

Jillian couldn't help but wonder when her mother's maternal wings had sprouted. Obviously, it had been late in life because there were no mental snapshots of the two of them being mother and daughter for Jillian to recall from her childhood. Perhaps, this had something to do with Jillian's need to disqualify herself from her own daughter's life. In many ways, she knew that she was ill-prepared for the job. Maybe she was running away from the task of mothering.

Cut from the Same Cloth

Throwing the wet dish rag into the sink, she watched clumps of pearly soap bubbles splatter onto the window just above the sink. Not only had she failed her daughter, but she had failed herself. Catching a glimpse of her daughter as she wiped down the window frame, the promise she made her baby girl on the day of her birth had been broken. Now it haunted her.

How could I have let you down? I promised I wouldn't do that to you, she thought.

As she watched her daughter through the kitchen window, she remembered the first time she held her child. Looking at her own reflection in the shiny kitchen window she could see herself as an exhausted young mother cuddling the new bundle swaddled in her arms. The memory was bittersweet.

It was there in the delivery room that she had promised her baby girl she would always be there for her. At that moment, she had meant every one of the words she had whispered in her new baby's ear, but before she knew it, she had become a carbon copy of her mother. Jillian had failed. Ashamedly, she had chosen to put her own well-being above that of her daughter.

She was truly sorry for neglecting Sam. No one knew better than she did how painful that could be. It was time to face the fact, she had been a terrible mother. Her only hope was that one day, maybe even today, she would find a way to turn their situation around.

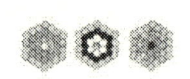

Laura Lea

*S*am had grown into a remarkably pleasant child. Prone to daydreaming, she was just like her father. She could have been his clone. Unfortunately, the only things Jillian had passed on to her daughter were her small frame and occasional moodiness. All in all, her daughter had acquired her parents' best traits.

Sam had missed out on so many important things growing up without a father. Yet, even though her life had been anything but normal, for a nine-year-old, she seemed well adjusted. Part of this was to Sam's credit, she was exceptionally resilient. Jillian knew, too, that without Gommy, Sam wouldn't be the child she was.

When Sam was two years old, her father, Peter, died in a tragic accident. Since then, Jillian had shied away from becoming emotionally attached to anyone, even her own daughter. She and Peter had been so close, and his sudden death had taken its toll on her emotions. For the first time in her life, she had experienced unconditional love, only to have it stolen from her. The hurt she experienced was so severe that she promised herself that she would never allow anyone to hurt her that way again. So, at the expense of the two people who loved her most, she built a very sturdy wall around her heart, refusing to let anyone pass through.

As Sam got older, she began to ask direct questions about her father, each one piercing Jillian's heart. Even though she longed to share with Sam so many stories about her father, she just couldn't bring herself to do it.

Eventually, Jillian decided to resurface. Just about the time she began to feel like opening up, Sam stopped asking questions. Emotionally, she felt strong and was ready to put Peter's death behind her. The

Cut from the Same Cloth

time had come for her to move on. Hopefully, one day soon she would have an opportunity to tell her daughter about her father. After all, it was his death that led to their present situation. It was the reason Gommy moved out to the farm.

Her presence in their home had provided a calm that Jillian was in no shape to provide. Joyfully, she had tackled the day-to-day tasks that were necessary to keep the household running. Sam had been drawn to her instantly, latching on like velcro. Anyone would have chosen Gommy's blooming disposition over that of her mother's somber state. Jillian had watched the bond between her mother and daughter grow deep and strong. There was little doubt the stability Sam needed was available to her in their circle of two.

There were times when Jillian wanted to jump right in and join them, but she didn't for fear that her presence might disrupt the delicate balance that existed between her mother and her daughter.

Gommy had literally saved their family, and Jillian was grateful for her mother's sacrifice. It couldn't have been easy for Gommy to give up her flower shop. It had been her life for over thirty years. Jillian never asked her to do it. She had done it on her own.

Jillian would never forget one of the many things her mother had told her after Peter died.

"Jilli, give yourself time. You can't rush a broken heart. Truth is, some of 'em never heal. I pray to God that your heart mends in time. Don't you worry though, I'll stay here with you and Sam as long as you need me."

Gommy had kept her word. The days had turned to years. Seven years, and counting, to be exact.

Laura Lea

Funny thing was, Jillian didn't know who needed her more. Was it Sam, or was she the one who so desperately needed her mother? There was no way Jillian could ever repay her mother for all that she had done.

Several times, when the subject had come up, Jillian remembered her mother saying, "Jilli, you don't owe me a thing. This is what grandmothers do. Don't you remember?"

Jillian did remember. Her very own grandmother had been her closest friend when she was younger.

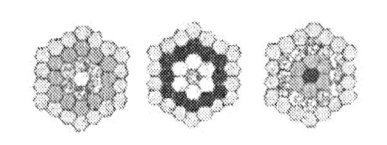

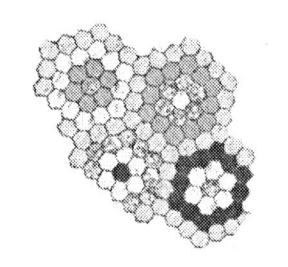

Chapter 8
For the Love of Flowers

Until last year, Gommy had been an active sixty-seven-year-old with a green thumb and silver hair. Her rather tall frame made her look all the more elegant as she carried herself about town. Gommy was obsessed with flowers. An avid collector, she had flowered hats and sheets, table cloths, and vases. If an object was in any way, shape, or form related to flowers, Gommy wanted it for her collection.

Around town she was known for her brightly colored clothing and love of flowers. Always dressed as though she was headed to church, she refused to leave the house without first styling her hair and painting her face and lips. She wouldn't be caught dead without her floral hair pins, her Blushing Beige face powder and a fresh coat of Crushed Petals lipstick. The funny thing was that she even felt the need to 'put on her face' and pin up her hair when she was working around the house or in her garden.

Cut from the Same Cloth

It wasn't that she was vain, because she wasn't. She just wanted to look her best.

"You never know when someone might drop by unannounced, and I wouldn't dream of embarrassing you by looking a mess," she would say. As she predicted, visitors stopped by often looking for gardening advice or gossip.

Gommy had been in Providence for forty-five years and was well known in the community. Admired by everyone for her ability to make things happen, she was a self-made businesswoman.

Back when the cotton mill closed, more than one hundred people lost their jobs, including Gommy. Figuring it would be almost impossible to find another job, she created one for herself. That's when The Garden Party was born. After spending years working at the mill doing a job she really didn't enjoy, she decided to strike out on her own. Hoping to turn her love of flowers into an income, she opened the first flower shop in the entire county.

With all of her savings and a business loan from the bank, she transformed the front three rooms of her home into a quaint little shop packed with flowers and plants. Seeing that her inventory was a little lacking, she tried to fill in the gaps by offering items from her personal collection for sale. There were vases and baskets, aprons and flower pots. She hated to part with some of them, but it was necessary if she was going to establish her business.

As the town's economic situation improved, so did her profits. The Garden Party became wildly popular. A perfect place to gather, Gommy kept a plate of Snickerdoodle cookies and a jug of lemonade on the front counter. Eventually, she became known around the county as the sole authority on flowers.

Laura Lea

She had done exactly what she wanted to do. She had turned a life long passion into a very successful business.
Over the years, other flower shops opened but Gommy never felt threatened. She was sure there was plenty of work to go around.
"Every day babies are born, and old folks die. Between the two, a whole lot of life can happen. May as well celebrate with flowers."
That had become her motto, *Celebrate With Flowers!*
She had been happy with everything that had happened with her business over the years, with the exception of the glass gazing ball craze. Wanting to take advantage of the sales opportunity, she stocked a large assortment of glass gazing balls. Some were elegant, some were fun, but all were breakable. Before she finally gave up on them, she had lost more to unattended children than to their parents. Several times she considered putting up a warning sign. Her new mantra was *You Can Eat, You Can Drink, But No Children Allowed!* Then her own three-foot-tall tornado would come by for a visit and do her share of damage. Eventually, Gommy wised up and got rid of the fragile orbs.
The Garden Party had been located at Fifth and Main since it opened, making it the cornerstone of the town square. This alone was enough to make Gommy famous. Several similar businesses had come and gone, but not The Garden Party. Not only had it survived, but it had flourished over the years, maintaining its cornerstone status.
Even with all of the store's unique inventory, Gommy's real claim to fame was her cutting garden and seasonal flower arrangements. Many young men would spend an entire Saturday morning roaming

Cut from the Same Cloth

through the cutting garden in search of the perfect flowers to fill a vase or corsage. Gommy loved this, even encouraged it, saying young love was good for business.

She loved her cutting garden. At first, it had been her way of saving money, but over the years it had become an essential part of her business. She would occasionally pick up new types of seeds and sprinkle them in a patch anxiously waiting for the buds to form. At that point, they were hers for the picking.

There were always daisies and mums, gourds and pumpkins. Mixing color and texture, her designs were as creative as they were beautiful. It was not uncommon for people to bring her bird nests and pine cones to include in her arrangements. Over and over, there was no end to her creativity.

The Garden Party had been her life. Never in her wildest dreams had she suspected there might be something out there that she would love doing even more.

Then, some years ago on a cold, icy morning in late February, the tragic death of her son-in-law, Peter, forced her to choose between a life that she had always known and one that she had only imagined.

Knowing her daughter would need her, she closed her flower shop and retired. After discussing the situation with Jillian, Gommy moved in with Jillian and Sam.

For a while, she couldn't decide what to do with her Aunt Sophia's house. Having been in the family for over a hundred years–first belonging to Uncle Earnest's parents, then Aunt Sophia and Uncle Earnest–selling it was out of the question. Gommy had always thought of it much in the same way as she thought of her quilts. It, too, was a family

Laura Lea

heirloom. Rather than sell the house, she decided to rent the space to her old friend and beauty operator, Betty Jean Sanders.

B. J., as Gommy called her, had been looking for a suitable place to house a beauty salon. After waiting for over a year, she had just about given up hope when Gommy called her with a proposition.

The news so excited B.J. that in less than thirty minutes, she was knocking on the front door of The Garden Party with her check book in hand. Having been a regular customer of Gommy's over the years, B.J. was familiar with the layout of the house. Immediately, her mind began to whirl.

"Gommy, this is perfect," B.J. squealed, obviously ecstatic over the possibilities. "I think I'll put the manicure station in the dining room and the reception area in the front study."

Standing in the main entrance hall, B.J. was a sight to behold. Even with her carrot-colored hair teased into a whale spout on the top of her head, she was still not five feet tall. Wearing her signature outfit, black spandex pants, white smock, hot pink scarf knotted at the neck, and faux leopard skin print bifocals dangling on her chest, she was the picture of self-confidence. Except for the neon pink lipstick and liner, she looked like a kid in a candy store.

"My word, Gommy, this place is going to be *the talk of the county*," she said, her hands clasped together beneath her chin. "You don't mind if I change the color, do you?"

"Let me guess," Gommy grinned. "Pink."

"How on earth did you guess that?" she asked, grinning from ear to ear. "I've got big plans for this place! I can see it now, people are going to come here

Cut from the Same Cloth

from all over to get *the works*," she insisted, making her way gingerly to the back door.

Peering through the square piece of lace that covered the window on the back door, she announced with great pleasure, "I'm going to need more parking."

At that, Gommy's mind turned from B.J. to the cutting garden out back. "It's always been there, you know," Gommy added, as if she was lost in thought. "I guess it would be alright, if you really think you'll need the room."

"Oh, there's no need to pave it, just some good old gravel will do the trick. I can use the rear door as an entran—."

Before the tiny hairdresser finished her thought, she realized how insensitive she had been. In one very long-winded breath, she had covered over a Providence landmark with a truckload of pea gravel.

The look of shock on Gommy's face quickly faded to sadness. The cutting garden had belonged to Sophia first, then to Gommy.

"Cover over the cutting garden?" she mumbled, trying to envision her beautiful blooms shrouded in dirty grey.

Sorry that she had offended her friend, as well as her future landlord, B.J. stood silently. For a moment, the only sound that could be heard was the echo created as B.J. feverishly smacked her gum.

"Well, I'll work out something with the city, maybe we can use the lot at City Ha—."

"No, B.J., it'll be fine. Might take me a while to get used to the idea, but really, it's okay. I'll be okay," Gommy said as though she was just now realizing the full extent of her sacrifice.

After a brief discussion as to the salon's set up, the two ladies settled on the monthly rent and sealed the

Laura Lea

deal with a cup of lemonade and a plate of Snickerdoodles. Before the crumbs were washed from the plate, B. J.'s mind had totally remodeled the place to fit her personality. Two months later, the actual work was complete, and The Swan opened for business.

※ ◎ ※

*F*or the first few months, Gommy's new life had been a strain. Peter's death was still fresh, and Jillian's tears fell constantly. To make matters worse, Sam was going through the terrible twos.
"What have I gotten myself into?" she would occasionally confide to her friend, Rose.
Many times Gommy questioned the wisdom of her decision to retire and move in with her daughter, only to realize that she had been granted the elusive second chance to be a mother. Eventually things settled down, and just like a new mother, she was free to rejoin the community again.
Thursdays at the Parker house had become known as Gommy's day off. Every Thursday was spent exactly the same way. She would join her best friends, Rose, Iris, Daisy, and Fern for breakfast at the Breakfast in Bed Café.
Rose's nephew, Harold, and his wife, Marcie, were the owners of Providence's trendy, little restaurant. Marcie's love of antique beds and linens were the inspiration for the café's decor. Harold built benches from old head boards and foot boards, and Marcie took care of everything else. No matter what your style, there was a bed to suit your fancy.

Cut from the Same Cloth

The "old gals'", as Harold called them, were partial to the queen size sleigh bed in the back corner. It was covered with a beautiful yo-yo quilt, giving it the look of lace. Because Aunt Rose was Harold's favorite relative, he showered the ladies with special attention. As soon as they walked through the front door, he'd yell, "G'mornin, Aunt Rose, ladies. Could I bring you your breakfast in bed?" They would all pretend to blush and then take their seats in the back.

After a while, Harold realized that it was possible to set his watch by their arrival. Rain or shine, they walked through the front door every Thursday morning at 9:00 a.m.

One morning over eggs and bacon, Harold heard them debating the merits of planting perennials. That's when he got the idea for their nickname. The following Thursday they were welcomed at their quilt covered table with a small sign that read, *Reserved for the Perennials*.

Aunt Rose and her friends adored their new nickname, thinking it to be very clever on Harold's part. Pretty soon word got out, and the whole town started calling them by their new name.

The five of them were dearest of friends. They all met when they were in their early twenties at the cotton mill. Since then, they had been close. There had been bumps along the way but, all in all, it had been a good ride. Their friendship, though tested several times, had survived longer than all of their husbands. Even after all they had been through over the years, they still enjoyed each other's company.

Conversation had always come easy for them. They frequently talked for hours, discussing every subject freely. There were some topics they had

Laura Lea

discussed so many times there was nothing new to add.

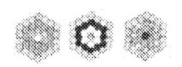

※ ◎ ※

*T*hree years ago, Fern and her husband, Charley, moved to Memphis to be near their grandchildren. Several times the Perennials had discussed visiting Fern and Graceland. Everyone wanted to go except Daisy.

"There ain't no way I'm going anywhere near that Graceland. Elvis might jump out from behind a bush and give me a heart attack!" As usual, when the topic of Elvis came up, they would all just look at her like she was nuts.

"I've done told ya'll, Elvis is alive, that whole death thing was just a plot to keep him from having to pay his back taxes. He's a make'n out like a bandit, too. I, for one, am not going to give him one penny of my social security check."

The only topic other than Elvis that they rarely seemed to get to was the topic of death. Actually, it wasn't death, because they did talk about it when it happened to other people. It was death, as it pertained to the four of them, that was the topic they didn't want to discuss.

Secretly, they all thought about it, even wondered who would go first. At one point, they would have all bet their life savings that it would be Daisy. After suffering a heart attack at the age of fifty-seven, she was at death's door for several weeks. Then one day, she sat up in bed and with tears in her eyes, yelled, "I

Cut from the Same Cloth

just saw Elvis. He was wearing a white robe. Is it too late to take that bus trip to Graceland?"

After Daisy's scare, they all decided it might be helpful if they each planned their funeral. So one afternoon over cheese pizza and sweet tea, they each set out to plan their own funeral. They made lists of songs and Bible verses. There was great debate over which clothing was the most flattering, and they even went as far as to plan the menu for the post funeral feast. When it was all said and done, Iris was the only one who felt it necessary to change her burial outfit, preferring the comfort of her cream colored pant suit to the elegance of her periwinkle Sunday dress.

"If I'm gonna have to wear it for the rest of my life you better believe I'm gonna be comfortable," and that was all she cared to say about the matter.

Talking about death shouldn't have been a big deal for the ladies. After all, they had known each other for going on fifty years. Maybe that was the problem. It was just too difficult to even contemplate life without one another. Sooner or later, however, they all knew they would have to face it.

After breakfast each Thursday, the Perennials would head over to the Bread of Life Food Pantry to sort and stock the bags and boxes of donations. Volunteering there had been an eye opening experience for Gommy. She had never before realized there were so many people in Providence who needed help from time to time. She knew the drought had been hard on the farming families. Many of them had been without any income for several months. For some of them, the food pantry was their only means of feeding their families.

Feeling compassion for them, Gommy and her friends would fill grocery bags with instant grits and

Laura Lea

macaroni and cheese, peanut butter and canned tuna hoping to give them enough food to last a few days.
    Being a volunteer at Bread of Life had been a humbling experience. In the eyes of every mother that came in for help, she saw her own mother. Growing up in a very poor family, there were many nights when she was sure the food on their table was there because of someone's generosity.
    She was learning late in life, what her parents had learned back when she and her siblings were small. It was true, sometimes people found themselves in situations beyond their control, and they had no choice but to ask for help. Her father had swallowed his pride for the sake of his family, and every day she watched as other men did the same thing.

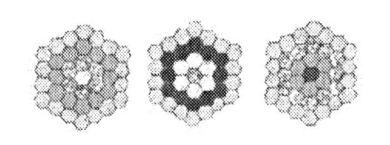

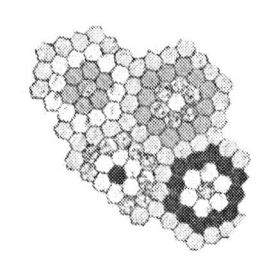

Chapter 9
Gommy's Decline

Gommy had been retired from the flower business for just over seven years when she slipped on a wet stepping stone in her garden and broke her hip. The surgery to repair the broken bone had gone well, but her recovery had been a different story.

A series of complications led to a second surgery, followed by a slow moving rehabilitation. To make matters worse, a condition known as congestive heart failure had surfaced during her recuperation. No one in their wildest dreams would have predicted that a lady with her spunk would get caught in a downward spiral and be unable to break free. It was as if a storm cloud had stalled above her. She could find no shelter from its rain.

A series of unfortunate medical problems slowed her recovery even further. First, there were painful muscle spasms, then a blood clot developed. When she was finally able to get up and move around, winter's chill had set in making her a prisoner in her

Cut from the Same Cloth

own home. Even if she had felt like going outside, the unusually cold weather would have kept her from doing so.

Everyone tried to encourage her to look forward to spring and its warmer weather.

"Mom," Jillian had said, "when the weather warms up, we'll get out and you can work in your garden." But, when the weather finally warmed, Gommy still needed her cane when she left the house, and her heart was weak.

Jillian was stunned by her mother's lack of determination. It just wasn't like Gommy to give up, but for some unknown reason, she didn't even try to push herself. Her doctor had tried different medications for her heart but nothing seemed to help. As Jillian watched her mother grow weaker, her own heart began to ache. For the first time in her life, she found herself trying to imagine life without her mother.

As winter waned, Gommy's energy returned. Yet with a weak hip and a heart that appeared to be utterly useless, her condition would improve for a few days only to deteriorate for the next three. It just didn't seem that she was making any progress.

Dependent on a cane, she was eventually able to take care of some of the household chores. Jillian didn't really need her mother's help, but she knew it made her feel useful.

As the days turned to weeks and the weeks to months, Jillian watched as her mother became both withered and frail. The only time Gommy wasn't bone thin was when her congestive heart disease caused her to swell up like a balloon.

No matter what her situation, she never complained. That was just not her style. She had

Laura Lea

learned to be content with her circumstances, believing with all her heart that something sweet would come from her suffering.

As far as Gommy was concerned, one of the most difficult aspects of her new life was accepting that she could no longer volunteer at Bread of Life. After several attempts to carry on with her work there, she was forced to admit that she was more of a hindrance than a help. Not only was the room too small for her walker, but it would be nearly impossible for her to dig through the boxes in search of pantry items. She would probably just hurt herself again or, even worse, someone else.

After the second surgery, she expected her life to return to normal within eight weeks, but six months had passed and she was still unable to live her life the way she had before her fall. The hardest part of it all was making peace with the notion that she would never be any better.

The Perennials came to visit often, and for that she was grateful. She loved their company and needed them now more than ever. She counted their friendship among her most prized possessions. They had never failed her, and she had put them to the test on more than one occasion.

Even though Gommy rarely left the house, she insisted on having her hair done once a week. Every Friday, B.J. Sanders would skip lunch and come by to wash and set Gommy's hair. These weekly visits did her a world of good. She felt better just knowing B.J. was coming over. Jillian was grateful that B.J. arranged her schedule to accommodate Gommy. Several times, Jillian had even tried to pay B.J. for her time, but being the kind of person that she was, B.J. refused the money.

Cut from the Same Cloth

"I couldn't take no money from ya'll," she'd say, smacking on a piece of bubble gum. "After all your momma did for me. You know, renting me the shop and all. So, you'll just have to keep your money, honey."

Except for her love of flowers, it seemed that Gommy had pretty much lost interest in everything.

"Sam," she recently said, "your mother bought me two packs of Cosmos seeds. Thought we might start us our own little cutting garden. Next time we get a good rain, I want you to sprinkle them on the bare spot out in front of my bedroom window."

"But, Gommy, you never let me sow your seeds before."

"I think you're gettin' big enough. Besides I can't get down out there and do it myself, now can I?" Gommy grinned as she pointed to the window in her bedroom. "You'll love these flowers. They sway and stretch, like they're dancing in the sunshine."

"Sure, Gommy, I can do it, but you'll have to show me where to strow'em."

"I will, but we'll have to wait 'til we get some rain. Right now the ground's too hard and more 'an likely the seeds would just blow away."

❖ ⬡ ❖

*U*ntil recently, taking care of Gommy had been easy. She could actually take care of herself and she did more than her share of the housework when her hip wasn't bothering her, but a month ago, she developed a nasty cold. Jillian hadn't been concerned until Gommy began to cough so severely that the

Laura Lea

muscles in her chest and stomach would cramp. Jillian tried several times to get her mother to go see Dr. Avery, but Gommy insisted the late winter cold would soon go away. It never did, and now she had pneumonia.

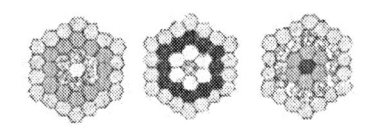

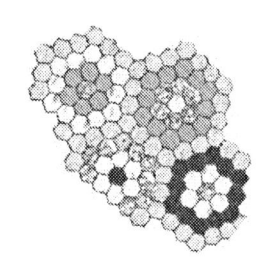

Chapter 10
Jillian

Jillian couldn't help but relive the events of the morning. She was glad Dr. Avery had taken the time to explain to her what was actually going on inside her mother's lungs. He wanted her to know what to expect if the infection didn't clear up. Jillian knew Dr. Avery would do all he could for Gommy, he always had, but even Jillian could see that his normally cheerful face had grown long and serious. She wasn't sure why, but she knew in her heart he didn't have good news. Even so, she was not prepared for what he had to say. His words had taken her by surprise, setting into motion events that would force her to reexamine her own past and future.

"Jillian, I've always tried to be honest with you."

Where have I heard that before? she thought.

"I have never felt it was right to give people false hope. Your mother's condition is quite serious. The pneumonia hasn't responded to the treatment like I had hoped."

Cut from the Same Cloth

"How much longer can she go on like this?" Jillian asked.

"Jillian, I can't answer that for sure. We've done all that we can do. I've tried several different medications, but nothing has made even the slightest improvement in her condition.

"Your mother's heart was already weak, and right now her body doesn't seem to be fighting the infection. It seems that the pneumonia's getting worse. I'm surprised that she has gone down hill so quickly. I was hoping she would be able to fight this. I'm sorry to have to tell you this," he said, his green eyes blinking to avoid welling with tears.

"I'll make sure that the nurses keep her comfortable. There's no reason for her to suffer."

He hated it when he had to do this. After all these years of practicing medicine, these kinds of talks were still difficult.

"Dr. Avery, are you saying my mother is going to...?"

Jillian couldn't even bear to think the word, much less say it.

Gommy, gone? How could this be happening?

Allowing herself a moment to let his words sink in, she realized this news was really not a surprise. Somehow, she had seen this coming.

The chasm between understanding that her mother was going to die and accepting that it might happen soon was too wide to cross at the moment.

Life without her mother. How on earth was that supposed to feel? What would she do without her mother? Gommy had been her rock for the last seven years.

After Peter died, it was Gommy she had depended on when the days were difficult. Jillian didn't know

Laura Lea

where she and Sam would be if it had not been for her mother.

With no regrets or second thoughts, her mother had given up her career and her home to move in with them. Did her mother know how grateful she was?

Hearing Dr. Avery's voice, she tried to focus once again on their conversation. Facing her, his unusually tall frame suddenly seemed shorter.

"Jillian, I'm really sorry. I wish I could tell you that she's going to get well this time, but I can't...I want you to be prepared."

"And how do I do that, Dr. Avery?" Jillian snapped. Turning to look away, she was embarrassed by her remark.

"I'm sorry, I didn't mean that." She knew he wasn't to blame, but he was a doctor. Wasn't he supposed to help her mother get well?

Sensing that Jillian might need a more private place to let all of this sink in, he gently took her by the arm and led her to a small consultation room beside the nurse's station.

"Why don't we sit in here so that we can talk in private?"

Collapsed into a striped wingback chair, Jillian sat quietly with her hands clasped in her lap. Staring into the eyes of a man who had been like a god to her, she couldn't believe what he was saying. He had always taken care of them when they were sick.

"Jillian, this can't be easy for you. I know you're close to your mother. I've always thought a lot of her myself. She's quite a lady, you know. If I could do something to help her get well, I would."

"I know, Dr Avery."

Cut from the Same Cloth

"But as her doctor, I've got to be up front with you. From a clinical standpoint, I don't think her chances are very good. On the other hand, if twenty-five years in medicine has taught me one thing it's that I don't really know a whole lot.

"So here's what we're going to do. We are going to pray that God will let us keep Louise here with us for a little while longer, and then we'll see just how anxious He is to move a new gardener up to Heaven.

"I don't want you to forget that unexpected things happen every day in medicine, most of which I wouldn't even begin to try to explain. I gave up trying to rationalize miracles years ago. You know, Jillian, when you get right down to it, there is very little that we actually get to control."

Looking into his weary eyes, Jillian knew he would have moved 'heaven and earth' to help her mother, but it just wasn't meant to be, not this time. So she said all she knew to say. "Thank you, Dr. Avery...for everything."

In all the years Jillian had known Dr. Avery, she had never thought to ask his age. She had assumed he was roughly the age of her mother. Today, however, he seemed older. Today, the fine lines around his eyes and the gray in his hair was clearly visible. He had been their family doctor for as long as she could remember. Jillian knew that he, more than most doctors, took situations like this personally. He was already grieving for his dear friend. It was clear that he cared about her mother, and she knew he cared about her and Sam, too.

Smiling sympathetically, he stood to leave. She could tell that he was truly sorry.

"Jillian, why don't you go home and spend some time with that daughter of yours?"

Laura Lea

"But, Doctor—?"

"Jillian, your mother's resting and I think you need to do the same. There's nothing you can do here. I'll call you if there's any change."

He turned to leave and, almost as an afterthought, looking back over his shoulder, said, "I know it's against hospital rules, but I'll let the nurses know that you may be bringing a young visitor when you return. Doctor's orders."

Winking, he turned and left the room.

Jillian sat for a moment allowing all that she had just heard to seep into her broken heart. Dr. Avery was probably right. She should go home and spend some time with Sam. After all, she was exhausted.

❖ ◉ ❖

*W*alking down the long hallway that led to the main entrance, she felt a strange sensation. It was as though she was being pulled by a magnet. Had someone called her name? Turning around, she looked back only to find an empty hallway. Slowly, she made her way back to Room 117.

Gommy was the magnet. With an inescapable force, she was pulling her daughter to her side. The self proclaimed ice princess had no choice but to get to her mother as quickly as possible.

Before entering her mother's room, she straightened her shirt and fluffed her hair. Without even thinking, she pulled a lipstick tube from her purse and reapplied a thick layer of Crushed Petals lipstick to her dry lips. Anyone watching the scene might have thought that a person of great fame was

Cut from the Same Cloth

waiting on the other side of the door. Filling her lungs with stale hospital air, Jillian slowly exhaled then quietly pushed open the door.

Unsure of what she would find, she entered the dimly lit room. Checking her watch, she saw that it was midmorning and yet, her mother's room seemed dark. As her eyes made the effort to adjust, her other senses seemed to sharpen.

Sounds that would ordinarily be too soft to hear were clearly audible. She could hear her mother's short breaths as they echoed around the warm room. There was also a sound that reminded her of water gurgling in a stream. Scanning the room, her eyes found the source of the sound. Attached to the oxygen port on the wall behind the bed was a bottle of bubbling water.

That must be the humidifier that Nurse Peggy was talking about the other day, Jillian thought. *How can she breath in this stifling air?*

The air felt thick enough to cut and smelled faintly of urine. There were soft, high pitched beeps coming from the machine by the bed.

Oh, Mom, she thought, *how can you stand this dreary room?*

Jillian wondered why the drapes were fully drawn. It was the first day in over a week that the sun had dared to show its face. Yet, her mother probably had no idea. It broke Jillian's heart to see her bright and cheerful mother lying in a bed with only a sliver of light pushing its way through the gap made by the carelessly drawn drapes. The depressing room made her wince. Surely her mother had not requested the drapes be drawn. That would have been so unlike Gommy.

Laura Lea

Jillian had been totally quiet until now. She glanced over at her mother's swollen body and for the moment would have sworn she was watching an angel taking a nap. It was hard to fathom that her mother could retain so much fluid. Just a week or so ago, Gommy was slim and frail. Now, she looked like she might burst at any moment.

Tiptoeing slowly across the greenish-grey tile floor, she reached the window, and with one hand slung the rose colored drapes apart only to be attacked by blinding sunlight. Squinting at the brightness, now she knew why the drapes had been closed. Gommy's room was on the eastern side of the building.

"Okay," she whispered, "you win. How 'bout we compromise?"

Jillian pulled the drapes in covering half of the window. "There, that's better," she said, approaching her mother.

"Hey, Mom, you awake?" She bent down to kiss her mother's forehead. "Wake up, sleepy head. It's me, Jilli. I came to see how you're doin'. You should see the sky this morning. It reminds me of the color of Mimi's hydrangeas. Do you remember them?"

Slowly, Gommy opened her eyes. Jillian was shocked at how blood streaked they were. Gommy blinked a few times as if she was trying to focus.

"Jilli, you came. Blue, they were blue."

Seized by the need to get rid of a clump of phlegm from her throat, Gommy coughed so hard that the motion righted her. Reaching to help her mother, Jillian grabbed a tissue from the bedside table to wipe the phlegm from her mother's chin.

"You alright, Mom?"

"Uh-huh," Gommy said while coughing.

Cut from the Same Cloth

"It's really warm in here. Are you hot?" Jillian asked, straining to see the thermostat that was attached to the wall opposite the bed. "I can lower the temperature a little if you want me to."

"I'm fine," Gommy whispered. "How's Sam? Miss her."

"She's fine. Dr. Avery said I could bring her in to see you this afternoon."

Then without any warning, Nurse Peggy breezed into the room.

"Good afternoon, ladies. How are you feeling, Miss Louise? Jillian, how long have you been here? I didn't see you come by the nurse's station."

"Hey, Peggy, I've been here awhile. You weren't at the nurse's station when I came by."

"Hmm, must've been down in the cafeteria on my break. They had Spanish omelettes and biscuits for breakfast this morning. Pretty good food down there, ever try it?"

"No, nothing except for coffee."

"Oh, well, I personally never touch the stuff. You know what with the rumors about caffeine an' all."

Turning her attention to the frail figure lying in the bed, Nurse Peggy, grabbed her little portable blue box, pushed its thermometer into a disposable sleeve, then gently slid it into Gommy's mouth. Jillian watched as her mother struggled to keep her lips sealed around the thin device.

"Sorry I have to do this, Miss Louise, just a few seconds long...there it goes," she said, pulling the thermometer from Gommy's mouth. "Okay, Missy, you're just a little bit warm. Think I'll talk to Dr. Avery, he may want to alter your medication."

While Nurse Peggy completed her tasks with the patient, Jillian moved to the window. The sky around

Laura Lea

the hospital was a picture perfect blue, but out over the horizon a band of angry clouds stood ready to storm their city. It was only a matter of time.
Oh, no, not more rain headed this way, she thought. She could hear Nurse Peggy talking sweetly to her mother. She had been the best nurse, really cheerful all of the time. It was obvious that she was crazy about older people.
 As she looked around her mother's room, Jillian saw it with new eyes, this time from a different point of view. She had been in this room several times, and saw it as nothing more than a temporary place for her mother to stay until she was well enough to come back home. Now that she had spoken with Dr. Avery, this small, stuffy cubicle had become her mother's private waiting room.
 But, what was she waiting for? Was she waiting to die or to live? Jillian knew her mother well enough to know the answer to her own question. Gommy was waiting to live.
 "Hon, I'm done here. I saw where Dr. Avery wrote a note for us to let that little girl of yours come for a visit with her grandma. I think that's a fine idea. I'd like to meet Sam. It is Sam, isn't it? I've seen all of the cards she's been makin' for Miss Louise. Seems like a thoughtful child. You gonna bring her by sometime today?"
 "Yeah, I thought I'd go home and do a little house work 'til she gets home from school. Then we can head on over."
 "My shift ends at 7:00 p.m. Hope you can make it back by then," Nurse Peggy said as she fluffed Gommy's pillow and straightened her covers. "Won't that be nice, Miss Louise? A little young blood on this hallway would make a lot of us feel better, but that's

Cut from the Same Cloth

just my opinion. I've been told on more than one occasion that nobody around here really cares about my opinion but me."

Slinging her stethoscope around her chubby neck in a show of defiance, she turned to leave. "I'll be back after a while, Miss Louise. Bye, Jillian."

Jillian wasn't sure, but she thought she recognized the look of sadness on the face of their usually cheerful nurse. Did Nurse Peggy know Gommy was dying?

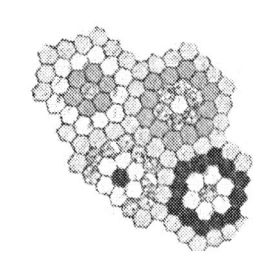

Chapter 11
Tears of Forgiveness

Moving to her mother's bedside, Jillian saw how gravely ill her mother looked. Almost without thinking she reached for the jar of Vaseline. Using a cotton swab from the bedside table, she smeared a small amount on her mother's dry, cracked lips.

"How's that, Mom?"

"Better."

Sitting there, holding her mother's puffy hand, she began to cry. As she traced the outline of her mother's fingers, streams of salty liquid dripped from her cheeks, each tear leaving a dark spot on her faded jeans.

Turning her head to better see her daughter, Gommy summoned her strength.

"Okay to cry, baby girl."

At the sound of those words, Jillian was unable to hold back her tears. Her mother had not called her that since she was a child. Gommy had even been known to call Sam "baby girl" sometimes. It was then

Cut from the Same Cloth

that the emotion Jillian had been trying to hold down could no longer be confined.

Rupturing the emotional dam, she had worked so hard to build, the years of pain and disappointment gushed forth. Her entire body began to shake as tears sprung from a source deep within her. Now, as she wept openly for her mother, she knew the abundance of tears was not just for Gommy. In fact, she was now crying for three generations of women, who had been pierced by the most difficult arrows life's bow could hurl, the loss of a true love and the need to belong.

As Jillian continued to stroke her mother's warm hand, she couldn't help but notice the thin silver wedding band that circled her own ring finger.

With her left hand, she removed her ring and read the inscription engraved on the inside.

"Forever," she whispered.

It did seem like it had been forever since he left them. A vision of her late husband came clearly into focus, his handsome, rugged face and green eyes, still perfectly clear in her memory. It was the Peter she saw sitting at the table with a bowl of Lucky Charms on the last morning of his life. He was running late and hadn't taken the time to shave.

Wondering what he would look like now, nearly ten years later, she tried to picture him. Would he look distinguished with salt and pepper hair or would he have the beginnings of a receding hair line? What did it matter? To Jillian, he would forever be young.

Pushing him from her thoughts, she focused her attention on her mother. Is this what her mother would want? Hadn't Gommy tried to convince her to deal with Peter's death, once and for all?

Laura Lea

Jillian could hear her mother's advice, words of wisdom shared during the difficult years after Peter's death.

"You've got to accept it, Peter's gone, and he's not coming back. I know this sounds harsh, but I understand what you're going through. Come on, honey, don't make the same mistakes I made. You have a daughter, who is very much alive, and she needs you. It's been long enough. You've got to let it go."

Looking at her mother's frail body, the time had finally come to let it go.

"Oh, Mom, maybe you've been right about all of this," she whispered. "It wouldn't be the first time. You'd think after all these years I'd get it through my thick head. Peter's not coming home. And yes, I know he didn't mean to fall. I just don't think I'll ever understand why all of this had to happen to me, to us.

"Oh, Mom, we were so happy, we had everything. I had everything."

As if the weight of her last thought had landed squarely atop the play button on the video player in her mind, she was forced to watch as Peter ate a quick bowl of cereal on their last morning together. She could see herself as she fed Sam her oatmeal. Their conversation had been ordinary.

"How cold is it going to get today, have you heard?" he asked.

"Not above freezing," she answered, wiping oatmeal from Sam's chin.

Jillian could barely stand knowing that their last moments together had been so...ordinary. In her mind, she saw herself wave to him from the kitchen window as he pulled out of their driveway. There she

Cut from the Same Cloth

stood, a telephone between her ear and shoulder, answering questions for a telemarketer with an oatmeal covered child in her arms.

"Oh, Mom, I never even told Peter goodbye. I was on the stupid phone when he left for work."

Sitting there, she could feel the familiar knot tightening in her belly. It was the one that always surfaced when her thoughts turned to Peter.

"If I had only known that he would walk out the door and never return, I would have done so many things differently. I would have made sure that he knew he had changed my life. Mom, until Peter came along, I never felt like I belonged to anyone. I would have told him I was grateful that we had a baby girl. There were no regrets."

Dropping her gaze from her mother to the floor, she whispered, "I never got the chance to tell him...goodbye."

Then, as her tears fell, Jillian felt her mother's heavy, swollen fingers rest upon her hand.

Even though Gommy's voice was raspy and soft, Jillian heard every word clearly.

"There, there." She coughed. "Now, dear, sweet Jilli." Her words were soft and breathy. "Go ahead, get it all out."

Leaning toward her mother, Jillian rested her head on her mother's chest. She could feel her mother stroking her hair. Moved by the tenderness of her mother's touch, she was a little girl again, small and helpless, allowing her mother to smooth away the hurt. As she continued to stroke Jillian's hair, Gommy spoke once again.

"Life's short...no guarantees—," She coughed. "Do...best you can, make...amends, so there's no re—"

Another cough.

Laura Lea

"...grets. I'm sorr—."
Again, she coughed.
"I got a se...cond chance. You might not. I nee...tell you...your fath—."
Seized by another coughing fit, Gommy was unable to finish her sentence.
Had Jillian heard her mother correctly? There had been so much coughing, her words had been difficult to make out. Jillian's eyes began to sting as a fresh well sprang open, releasing more salty tears onto her already tender eye lids. All of this time, her mother had been trying to make amends.
Is that what she was trying to say? Had her mother spent the past seven years trying to make up for being unavailable to her when she was a child?
All at once a new revelation hit her. *Maybe this isn't just about me, maybe it's about her, too.* Had her mother seized a rare opportunity and given parenting a second try? Is that what she was talking about when she spoke of second chances?
"Mom, all of this time, I thought you were helping me with Sam so that I could get back on my feet," Jillian whispered, looking directly into her mother's blood streaked eyes.
For the first time, since Gommy had gotten sick, Jillian realized her mother was going to die. Even now, she shuddered at the extent of her mother's decline. Gommy looked very old and fragile.
Most of Jillian's life had been lived with little attention from her mother, and even less from her father. Now that they were finally attempting to understand each other, to tear down the wall that had kept them apart, her mother was preparing to die. Heartbroken by the thought, Jillian determined that

Cut from the Same Cloth

she and Sam would have at least one more visit with the lady who had so touched their lives.

"I was," Gommy whispered, so softly that Jillian actually had to read her mother's dry, cracked lips.

"Was Sam your second chance? Is this what you meant?"

"Jilli, you still have time," Gommy said, her words soft but clear. "I made too many mistakes," she said weakly. "Don't you make them, too," Gommy said as though she were giving her daughter a command.

"Thirsty, Jilli,...water, please."

Reaching over her mother to the bedside table, Jillian picked up the large cup and lowered it to her mother, bending the straw and placing it in her mother's mouth. Staring at the straw, she watched the water level rise as her mother sipped the cool liquid.

"Thank you,...was thirsty," Gommy said with a slight smile as she watched her daughter place the cup back on the table.

With a peaceful silence draping the room, Jillian couldn't help but replay her mother's words in her head. Then without any warning, Jillian's tears came quickly, her whole body involved in the effort. Realizing she was crying far too loudly, she tried to get her emotions under control. Yet, why did she feel that was necessary? Hadn't her mother encouraged her to get it out?

As if her mother knew exactly what she was thinking, she spoke. "Jilli,...long time ago, you need—"

She was seized by more coughing.

"...to move on, must forgive him, it's time. Before it's...late for you...or Sam"

"Forgive Peter," Jillian said defensively. "Why do I need to forgive Peter?"

Laura Lea

Jillian could feel a tinge of resentment rising in her, an anger bubbling deep within. Feeling her body stiffen, she was unable to control the anger that had been smoldering for years. From somewhere deep inside, a violent eruption occurred, shooting her from her chair. Needing to move, she paced the small room.

With her fists clenched, she hurled angry words at a husband who was unable to defend himself. For the first time in seven years, feelings she had been too ashamed to admit flew from her mouth, surprising even her.

"Oh, Peter, how could you have been so careless? You knew how dangerous it was to be on the roof of that building in freezing weather."

It was Peter who had robbed her and her daughter of the life she had longed for.

"How could you, Peter? You promised to take care of me, of us. We depended on you. And you let us down! You let Sam down."

Even though she cried loudly, she knew that Peter could not hear her. For the first time, the words that spewed from her heart reached her ears. Standing in the dimly lit room, with tears streaming down her face, she could feel the weight lifting from her shoulders.

Surprised by the thoughts that had so eagerly surfaced, Jillian crumpled into her chair, her heart pounding in time with the ticking of the wall clock above the bed.

Noticing the time, she knew she would have to leave soon if she wanted to be back home before Sam returned from school. Not wanting to leave her mother's side, she was torn between their new bond

Cut from the Same Cloth

and wanting to get home, so that she could bring Sam for what might be her last visit with Gommy.

Back beside her mother, she crumpled into the chair, totally exhausted from the emotional strain of the morning.

What could she say to this woman who had done the best she could over the years? Wanting to be profound, the only words she could think to say were, "I'm sorry." And she truly was.

Gently stroking her mother's silver hair, she knew it was time to go. "Mom, I'll be back soon with Sam, you rest now, okay?"

Bending slightly, she kissed her mother's forehead, then turned toward the door. Reaching for the door knob, Jillian turned to look at her mother one last time. It was then that she saw her mother's tears.

"Sorry, too, baby girl."

Had Jillian heard her correctly? Her mother's voice had been so soft and raspy.

"Oh, Mom," Jillian cried, moving quickly to her mother's bedside.

Reaching for her mother's hand, Jillian was overcome with a warmth she had never known. Never in a million years had she dreamed that she and her mother could become so close. In what seemed like only minutes, years of hurt and regret were gone, melted from her once frozen heart.

Shaken by another coughing fit, Gommy's whole body seemed to be trying to rid her chest of the massive infection. Jillian tried to help her mother, but it seemed pointless. She couldn't help. No one could.

Once Gommy was calm again, Jillian took her mother's transparent hand into her own. Focusing on her mother, Jillian recalled the words Gommy had

Laura Lea

spoken earlier about life being short and making amends.

Even with Gommy's hazel eyes closed, small pools of liquid still formed in their corners. Opening her mouth to speak, Jillian interrupted her, gently placing her fingers on her mother's lips to prevent her from speaking.

"No, Mom. Please, just listen. I've got a few things I need to say. Thank you for today. You gave me a mother today. Even if we don't have much time left, this is what I will remember. And, for Sam, I couldn't have taken care of her. What would I have done if you hadn't been willing to help me with her? She's quite a girl, and it's all because of you.

"I've been watching all of these years, and you know what, I think I can do this. I think I can be a good mother, you taught me how. I won't forget all that you've done for us, for me.... Mom, you gave up so much for us."

"That's what mothers do," Gommy whispered.

Looking deeply into her mother's eyes, Jillian could see the tears spilling onto her ashen, puffy cheeks.

"There's no way for me to repay you," Jillian whispered.

Jillian watched as her mother's ears filled with the salty tears. Using the hem of her soft cotton shirt, she dabbed the liquid pools until they were dry.

"Oh, Mom, I promise you I'll take care of our girl. We'll be okay, I promise. Why don't you try to sleep? I'll be back soon with Sam."

As Jillian stood to leave, she sensed relief on her mother's face. Maybe it was her imagination, but she didn't think so. Closing the door behind her, she noticed her mother's name written on the clipboard

Cut from the Same Cloth

that hung on the peg by the door. *Black, Louise* it read. Touching the letters with her fingertips, she mouthed her mother's name.

"Hold on, Mom, just a little longer."

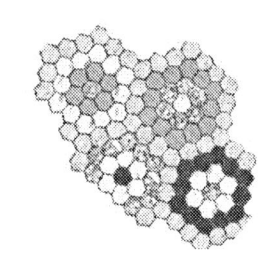

Chapter 12
Making Peace At Last

*S*itting in her van, in the hospital parking lot, Jillian's mind was spinning in several directions. Desperately, she wanted to make sense of what had happened this morning. In just a short time, her entire world had been turned right-side up.

The mother, who had neglected her as a child, was now dying and Jillian would do almost anything to have more time with her. The husband, who had saved her from a life of isolation, had been the reason for her inability to reach out. Most importantly, it would soon be necessary to ask her daughter to give her a second chance at being a mother, even when there was no sane reason for Sam to do so.

How did my life get so screwed up? she wondered as she turned the key in the ignition.

Pulling out of the parking lot, her thoughts turned to Peter. His death had been a weight holding her just below the surface of life. All around her people had been living life with all of its highs and lows. For too

Cut from the Same Cloth

long she had been numb, just going through the motions.

Until today, she hadn't really cared very much about really living. For seven years, she had been unable to bring herself to try to solve her problems, afraid of what she might find. It was a severe case of unresolved anger that had kept her from living. Instinctively, her mind went to Sam.

Oh, Sam, you've missed so much because of me. I hope I'm not too late.

Breaking through her daughter's tough shell would be difficult. There were many apologies to make and hours of time to make up for.

Driving along Main Street, she thought of her poor mother lying in a hospital bed preparing to die. What would she and Sam do without her? They had both come to depend on her for so many things.

Jillian had to hand it to her mother, she had taken her second chance at motherhood seriously. Was it possible to fill her mother's shoes? Could her daughter ever find it in her heart to give her a second chance?

That was the question. Once Gommy was gone, Sam would have no choice. She would have to accept her mother. Would Sam be receptive to the idea? There was no way to know until the time came.

There were so many issues to set straight. First and foremost was the task of getting to know her daughter. She found it difficult to fathom that seven years had passed. She and Sam had a great deal of catching up to do. She also needed to help her daughter learn more about her father. Her own memories of Peter were crystal clear. One day, soon, she would share them with Sam.

Laura Lea

As she drove through town, Jillian was amazed at how free she felt. The tears that she shed that morning had cleansed her soul. Glancing to the right, she saw *The Swan*. Gommy's house was now a thriving beauty salon.

As she sat by her mother's side, Jillian had seen how truly beautiful she was. It wasn't a physical beauty, even though Gommy had always been a lovely lady. It was an inner beauty, a beauty that comes from knowing you've done your best. Even though her mother did look pale and puffy, there was something about her that was warm and inviting.

Suddenly, the realization that the time she had left with her mother was short hit her right in the gut. Her mother was dying, and they had precious little time left. Gasping for air, she thought she might hyperventilate.

A new whirl wind of thoughts began to spin inside her head.

Mom, you're going to leave me too, aren't you? First Dad, then Peter, and now you. What will I do without you?

Her mother had been responsible for so much that happened on a daily basis.

Who will help us, if you're not here? Who will I turn to for advice?

Once again, she was coming undone, and she hated the feeling. What had happened to her new sense of hopefulness?

"Just stay calm," she told herself as she took a series of deep breaths. She had to remain calm. She couldn't let Sam see her this way.

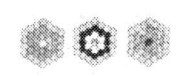

Cut from the Same Cloth

*F*inally at home, Jillian entered her mother's bedroom, a shrine to her mother's memory. All around her, displayed in every available spot were the pieces of her mother's life, mementos of all she held dear.

Walking to the dresser, she picked up a pewter picture frame that held a black and white photograph of her mother with the other Perennials. They were all smiles as they sat atop the back seat of an old, two-tone convertible. Many times over the years, she had tried to identify the driver of the car. Often wondering if it might be her father. Now she would never know.

Walking over to the bed, she fell back onto the Flower Garden quilt.

Gosh, Mom, this quilt's older than me, she thought.

Scanning the quilt, she immediately found her strip. With her fingers, she traced the stitches that held pieces of her old brownie uniform in place. Shimmering to the left was a beautiful sea foam green taffeta that she wore when she went to her senior prom. Continuing down the strip, she found a six-sided piece of her favorite flannel gown. Her mother had worn one just like it.

At the very end of the strip, a frayed white eyelet hexagon clung to the quilt. Jillian didn't personally remember wearing the garment from which it had been cut, but according to her mother, it was a remnant from the christening gown they had both worn when they were babies.

With both arms outstretched, she tugged on the quilt drawing it around her in a warm hug. It had a softness that could only come from worn fabrics. Breathing in, the smell of roses was so strong, she gasped for air. Jillian had never cared for their heavy

Laura Lea

sweet scent, but rose water had long been her mother's favorite fragrance.
 Wrapped in the worn, soft, cotton quilt, Jillian was comforted by its warmth. Even though, she knew she was alone, she didn't feel lonely. Being in her mother's room wrapped in the quilt that told the story of her mother's life, she felt at peace. The uncertainty of what lay ahead was something she would tackle when the time came. For now, she was content to be near her mother any way she could.
 As she lay on her mother's bed, she caught a glimpse of Sam's school picture in a simple wooden frame, sitting amongst the knick-knacks on her mother's dresser.
 Sam, she thought, *how will I convince you to let me be a part of your life? You've always relied on Mom.*
 Suddenly, Jillian would have sworn she heard her mother's voice. Shaking her head as if she was trying to remove something from her mind, she heard her mother's words again.
 God is with you.
 If she could ask for advice from her mother at this very minute, she knew exactly what her mother would tell her to do. It was Gommy's solution to everything. Pray.
 Her mother had been right about Peter, she was probably right about this, too. Dropping to her knees beside her mother's bed, she was a child again. With her head bowed, and palms pressed together, she began to pray.
 Silently, thoughts poured from her heart to a god that she had never trusted or tried to understand. At first, she didn't know what to say. It had been years since she had even thought about praying. It felt

Cut from the Same Cloth

strange to her, but she did it anyway, knowing her mother would have done it, too.

As she began to speak her mind, she felt like a child, utterly dependent. Was that the point? She was a little girl, innocently asking for help from the only one who really could. With nowhere else to turn, she had nothing to lose.

"Oh, God," she whispered, her words sounding unfamiliar.

Opening her eyes just slightly, she quickly closed them, thinking that God wouldn't appreciate such disrespect. Unconsciously going through the motions, she heard herself say, "I need you."

The words struck her as odd, she knew she needed her mother, but God...He had never been there for her before. Instantly, her mind was filled with words she wanted to say. For the second time today, she had no control over the words that flew from her mouth. Her heart contained thoughts she didn't want to claim.

Questioning whether God was even listening to her, she could feel the tension begin to rise. Before she could stop herself, words began to spew from her lips.

"Can You help us? Will You help me? God, please, don't take Mom. You don't need her, but I do, and Sam does, too. Please, God, You are our only hope. Dr. Avery said so. I'll do whatever You want me to do. What do You want me to do? WHAT IS IT THAT YOU WANT FROM ME? Oh, God, please, just let her live. I need her."

As tears began to fall from her eyes, she bent over, cupped her hands over her face, and wept. Then, as if she could no longer contain the bitterness welling up inside her heart, it spewed with such force that she hardly recognized her own voice.

Laura Lea

"You knew I needed Peter, and You still let him die. You could've saved him. Please, don't take Mom, too. You can save her. Why are You doing this to me? What did I do to deserve this? Who will I—?"

Then from out of nowhere, she heard her mother's voice. It seemed so real she looked around to see if someone had entered the room.

Alone. She was alone, yet she was positive she heard her mother's voice whispering in her ear. Her words were familiar. Jillian had heard them often through the years.

God is with you.

For her entire life, the words had seemed hollow until now. Now, she had no choice but to believe them. Just when she thought there were no tears left, a new well sprang to life, stinging her already swollen eyes.

"Oh, God, please, don't leave me. Everybody keeps leaving me. First, Papa, then Mee-Maw, Peter, and now Mom. Sam is all I have left, and I don't even know if she wants me around. I do need You. Maybe I always have."

Jillian couldn't believe what she was saying. Yet, in her heart she knew it was the truth. For the second time this morning, she was being pulled.

This time, however, God was the Magnet. Maybe God *could* be trusted. Maybe He *had* been with her all of this time. Had she just chosen not to believe?

During the past seven years, her mother had been God's hands, constantly working to protect and nurture her and her daughter.

It was Gommy who had been teaching Jillian how to cope all of these years. She had been preparing her for the day that would soon be here. Jillian knew her

Cut from the Same Cloth

mother would have considered her task a labor of love.

For a moment, she sat perfectly still. "Mom, is this what you've been trying to tell me?"

Afraid to make any noise for fear she wouldn't hear God's voice should He choose to speak, she sat quietly in her mother's room. No longer afraid of the dark days ahead, she was amazingly calm. Her tears had come and washed away the anger that had prevented her from living all of these years.

For the first time, since Peter's death, maybe in her whole life, the world didn't feel so lonely. God was with her and He would never leave.

If her mother didn't survive, she was ready to face death again. Maybe she was finally beginning to learn the lessons death had come to teach. She had spent her entire life depending on other people for help and happiness. First, Peter, then her mother. From now on, she would depend on God.

Jillian sat for a few moments drying her eyes with the cuffs of her shirt. She couldn't explain it, but she felt relieved. Finally, the pieces of her life were starting to fit together like one of her mother's quilts.

❈ ❖ ❈

As she stood to leave her mother's room, she recognized a small photo on the shelf of the curio cabinet. It was a picture of an older lady with light-colored hair and wire-rimmed glasses, sitting in a rocking chair holding a curly haired youngster. She didn't recall ever seeing the picture before. She wondered who the two people were. If she hadn't

Laura Lea

known better, she would have thought the little girl was Sam, but the picture was far too old. Closing the door to Gommy's room, she realized who the people in the photo were. Leaning against the door frame, her mind returned to Mee-Maw's house.
    The day was overcast, hot, and muggy. Sitting Indian style on the concrete stoop by her Mee-Maw's back door, Jilli tried her best to eat the deep purple slushy from the paper cup without dropping the sticky liquid on her blue-checked sundress. Mee-Maw's frozen grape juice was little Jilli's favorite summer time treat. Sweet like candy, it was refreshing on a hot summer day. By the time, she reached the bottom of the cup, her mouth was so cold she could barely move her lips.
    The morning almost gone, Mee-Maw worked quickly to get the wet towels and sheets clipped to the nylon rope Pawpaw had strung between two rusty metal poles in the back yard. Singing to pass the time, Mee-Maw's rich soprano voice was strong and clear. Jilli listened as her grandmother serenaded the wet laundry with the hymns of her faith. Amazingly, the breeze began to stir, flapping the wet fabric in a round of applause.

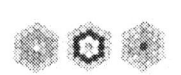

❄ ✪ ❄

    Dumbfounded by the ability of an old picture to transport her back in time, Jillian was curious about what else she might find among her mother's many treasures. Today, however, was not the day to explore

Cut from the Same Cloth

Gommy's room. There was laundry to catch up on and a kitchen to clean.

    Her morning was a blur. Not only had she spent a considerable amount of time with her mother, but she had also done some housework. It was a good thing that she was capable of working and thinking at the same time, because her mind had been extremely busy. Even while resting on the porch, she had been totally consumed with thoughts of her family. It was the slamming of the back door that shook her from her thoughts.

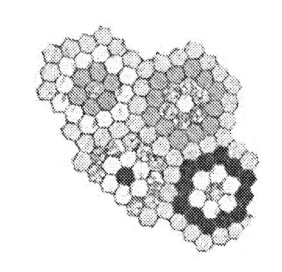

Chapter 13
Sam Learns the Truth

"Yippee," Sam yelled, slamming the back screen door. "Did you see it? Did you see me jump? Pretty cool, huh?"

"Um, yeah, I did," Jillian stuttered as her mind returned to the present. "I'd say dangerous is more like it."

"Oh, Mom, you worry too much, and besides, it's really not that dangerous."

"Well, it looked like it from here."

Jillian wasn't about to let Sam know that concern had prevented her from watching the now-infamous leap.

With no servants there to cater to her needs, the starving queen swung the door of the refrigerator open. Staring at its contents as though she was in a trance, she failed to hear her mother's command.

"Sam, did you hear me? I said go wash those filthy hands."

Cut from the Same Cloth

Snapping her fingers in front of Sam's face, Jillian finally got her daughter's attention.
Holding them up for inspection, Sam pretended her hands were already clean.
"But, Mom, they're not dirty," Sam sighed rolling her eyes.
Jillian glanced her way looking skeptical.
"Oh, alright," Sam fussed, "I know, I know. 'If I've told you once, I've told you a thousand times, you can't see germs,'" Sam sang, mimicking her mother.
Swatting at her daughter with a damp dish rag, Jillian teasingly chased her toward the bathroom.
"Don't forget to use soap," her mother called.
"Hey, Mom, is this clean enough for you?" Sam asked in a sarcastic tone as she bounced back to the kitchen. Waving her spotless, dripping hands in her mother's face, she flicked cool water in her mother's direction.
"Have we got anything to eat? I'm starving," Sam whined as she opened the refrigerator door.
"There's a bowl of grapes on the bottom shelf of the fridge," Jillian answered.
Holding the refrigerator door open while she searched for the grapes, Sam was momentarily cooled by the rush of cold air. Her eyes moved from shelf to shelf, in search of the grapes.
"Here they are," she said. Sliding the container out of the refrigerator, she set it on the counter and popped off the top. There, nestled in the center of what looked like a hand full of dead tape worms, was a large, furry glob of pink and grey.
"Ooh, gross, what *is* this stuff?" Sam grimaced holding it an arm's length away for her mother to examine.

Laura Lea

"Kinda looks like old spaghetti," Jillian said wincing at the sight. "Just put the whole container in the garbage."

"Mom, I thought you said we had some grapes," Sam whined.

"We do, I had some before you got home from school."

Jillian reached around Sam and, without even looking, pulled the grapes from the refrigerator.

How does she do that? Sam wondered.

Jillian poured the two of them a glass of milk and joined Sam at the table. Sam was the first to speak.

"Hey, Mom, did you go see Gommy this morning?"

"Yes, I spent most of the morning at the hospital."

"She's been gone so long, is she comin' home soon?"

"Well...Sam that's what I need to—."

"Hey, did I tell you I got a ninety-two on my math test today?" Sam interrupted grinning from ear to ear.

"Math test, did you have another math test today?" Jillian asked.

"No, Mom, it was yesterday."

"Oh, that's right. Lately, my days keep running together. Ninety-two, that's pretty good for somebody who says they can't do math."

Sam didn't like math, but lucky for her, it was Mickey's favorite subject. Sometimes her mother would let her invite Mickey over to play, and he would help her study if they had an upcoming test.

"I guess it really helped to have Mickey come over to study after all," Jillian teased.

As if she was fifteen years old again with her pom-poms in her hands, she belted out her Mickey chant.

"Oh, Mickey, you're so fine, you're so fine you blow my mind, hey, Mickey, hey, hey, hey,—."

Cut from the Same Cloth

"Come on, Mom, stop it...STOP IT! Don't do that. You know I hate it when people sing stuff like that. It's embarrassing."

"Alright," Jillian sighed pretending to throw pom-poms to the side. "I can't believe you don't like my Mickey chant."

"Well, I guess it's one of those had-to-be-there kind of things. I have another math test next week, and I bet Mickey's mom would let him come over to help me study if you called her."

"Maybe, we'll just have to see."

Jillian knew she had procrastinated too long. She needed to tell Sam about Gommy, but for the life of her she couldn't find the courage to do it. She wanted to tell her the truth. She always had, but this time she had a sick feeling in the pit of her stomach. Sam was going to be devastated, and Jillian wasn't sure if she would be able to help her deal with her grief.

Oh, Mom, I wish you were here, Jillian thought. *Sam listens to you. You'd be able to console her."*

If only she and Sam were closer, this wouldn't be so difficult. Jillian waited for a lull in the conversation hoping to gather her courage. Then, from out of the blue, Sam started the conversation for her.

"Hey, Mom, you didn't tell me about Gommy yet. When's she coming home?"

"Well, Sam, that's what I need to talk to you about."

"Did you take her the card I made? Did she like it?" Sam asked, full of questions.

"Yeah, I sat it on the side table so that she could see it."

"I can't wait for her to get home. I really miss her. She's been gone forever. I hate that stupid old hospital rule."

Laura Lea

"Come on, Sam, don't say that word. Can't you think of anything better to say?"
"Well, I do. It's not fair to keep kids out of the hospital. Anyway, I'll be ten on my next birthday."
"Last time I checked, you were closer to nine than you are to ten."
"Well, how are they gonna know how old I am anyway? Have they got the birthday police checking birth certificates? Besides, don't you think I look older than ten?"
Jillian wasn't going to fall for this trap. It didn't matter how she answered, Sam would take it the wrong way.
"Sam, that's not the point, the hospital rules are there to keep you from getting sick, and the patients from getting sicker. It makes sense whether you understand it or not."
"Maybe so, but it's still a stupid rule."
Jillian gave her daughter the dreaded 'evil eye' stare for using one of the forbidden words yet again.
Raising both arms in surrender, Jillian said, "Well the rule doesn't matter now anyway. Dr. Avery asked me, well, actually, he told me to bring you to visit Gommy. He thought having you there might make her feel better."
"No way!"
"Yes way."
"You mean I get to go to the hospital anyway?" Sam asked, nodding her head as if her debating skills had netted her a victory.
"So when can we go?" she said impatiently.
Jillian knew she would want to go right away, but she couldn't take her to visit Gommy without first telling her the truth. She wasn't sure how to prepare

Cut from the Same Cloth

her daughter for what was ahead. She wasn't even sure she was ready for it herself.

"We'll go soon, but first I need to talk to you about Gommy."

Remaining calm, Jillian took a deep breath releasing it slowly. She didn't know any other way to tell her, so she just repeated the words Dr. Avery had said to her earlier in the day.

Trying to sound hopeful, Jillian spoke softly, stopping often to give Sam time to let the words sink in. Sam listened quietly showing no obvious emotion. Jillian wished she knew what her daughter was thinking. It wasn't like Sam to be so quiet.

Sam was usually transparent, easy to read, when it came to matters of the heart. That was one of her best qualities, as far as Jillian was concerned. She wore her emotions on her sleeve. Jillian always knew where she stood with her daughter. This time, however, Sam was holding back. Remembering her own reaction earlier in the day, Jillian's heart ached for her daughter.

Give her time, she thought.

So, quietly, they sat on opposite sides of the kitchen table, each one trying to understand what was happening.

After a few minutes, Sam's eyes began to puddle with tears. The impact of her mother's words hit her all at once, causing tears to spill onto her freckled cheeks. Reaching for her mother, she was welcomed with open arms. Surprisingly, she felt a sense of calmness, even though the news of her grandmother unleashed a whirlwind of emotion. Bracing herself for the coming fall, she buried her face in her mother's shoulder. Tired from the heaving that an emotional

Laura Lea

cry often brings, calmness came after only a few minutes.

Sam couldn't remember the last time she sat in her mother's lap. Surely, she used to sit there when she was younger. Surprised at how warm and soft it felt to be nestled in her mother's arms, she couldn't help but think of her grandmother.

Gommy's lap was an old leather chair softened by years of use. Sitting together they would read and talk and sing. They both liked to sing, Gommy, hymns, and Sam, anything country. It had never really mattered what they did, it was the warmth of the closeness that made their time together memorable. Sam had never thought of her mother's lap as a comforting place to be, but maybe she had been wrong. Maybe her mother's lap could one day feel like an overstuffed recliner, warm and cozy.

Once her tears slowed, the heartbroken child managed to question her mother about Gommy.

"Is he sure she's really got that whatever you called it?"

"Pretty sure."

"Well, he doesn't know everything! Should we take Gommy to a different doctor?"

Sam's anger was beginning to surface, forcing her from her mother's lap. As the salty tears continued to sting her eyes, she made her way toward the window. Embarrassed by her own disrespectful outburst, she spun on her heels to keep from making eye contact with her mother.

"Sam, Dr. Avery's a great doctor. You've always liked him."

With her arms folded across her chest, she turned to face her mother. Choking on her words, Sam continued her inquisition.

Cut from the Same Cloth

"He can't let Gommy die. How did she get so sick, anyway? You said it was just a bad cold."

Sam's icy stare caused Jillian to shiver. The more Sam spoke, the louder she got. "Why didn't you take her to see him before she got so bad?"

Emotionally raw herself, Jillian's own temper flared.

"Now, you just wait one minute, young lady. I tried to get Gommy to go see Dr. Avery when she first got sick, but she wouldn't go."

Jillian hated what was happening. She hadn't expected Sam to blame her.

"You should have made her go. You make me go to the doctor when I don't want to. If you had, maybe this wouldn't...."

Catching herself before she hurled the final dagger, she no longer felt brave or courageous. Instead, Sam was now the villain, the one bent on inflicting pain. Ashamed of her behavior, she focused her gaze on the checkerboard tiles on the floor, unable to bear the hurt that must surely be visible on her mother's face.

Silently, as if they were mannequins in a store front window, they each held their pose. Sam was the first to move. Inching her head up a little at a time, her tear-streaked face met her mother's gaze. Facing her victim was difficult, yet she had no choice.

The anger that she had struggled with only moments earlier was fading with the realization that her mother would never harm Gommy. Her grandmother's condition was not her mother's fault. Yet, strangely enough, blaming someone else made her feel better.

"I'm sorry, I know it's not your fault," Sam admitted. Her mother would have done something if she could have. She was sure of that.

Laura Lea

With Sam's attitude beginning to soften, Jillian noticed her daughter's tear-streaked face no longer appeared pinched or pointed. Touched by her daughter's apology, she pulled the grieving child close. At first, her embrace was met with resistance. However, within minutes, the infamous Parker stubborn streak had met its match. The warmth of Jillian's arms quickly melted away Sam's icy resistance. For the first time in years, Jillian felt like someone's mother.

With her fingers, Jillian smoothed Sam's silky curls, allowing her daughter to grieve in her arms. It didn't matter that she had no idea what to say to her little girl, it was her presence that spoke volumes. After all, there were few memories from Jillian's childhood that she could draw from to help her deal with this, yet for the past seven years she had unconsciously observed her mother's ability to be selfless. Gommy had made it a point to give of her time. She gave it first to her family, then to her friends, and finally, to the charities that were close to her heart.

Once Sam was calm, Jillian felt free to speak.

"Sam, I don't want Gommy to die either," Jillian whispered continuing to gently rock her baby girl. "Shhhhh, its okay to cry. I'm here."

"Dr. Avery said it wouldn't hurt to pray for a miracle. He sees them from time to time," Jillian said reassuringly.

In her heart, she didn't hold out much hope, but for Sam's sake she had to be optimistic. Not knowing what else to say, Jillian held her daughter and let her cry.

Cuddled in her mother's lap, Sam whimpered. Not only were tears dripping onto her lap, but her

Cut from the Same Cloth

nose had begun to run as well. Without thinking, she raised her shirt tail and began to dry her face. Unaware of what she was doing, Sam blew her dripping nose into her shirt.

"Saaam," her mother scolded, handing her a napkin from the holder on the lazy susan.

Realizing what she had done, a smile slowly spread across her tear-stained face. For a moment, the two of them sat looking at each other. Tired of sadness and tears, slowly they gradually began to smile. Jillian was thankful for the diversion, even if there was a wad of nose yuck smeared on the hem of her daughter's shirt.

"Pretty gross, huh?" Sam said slightly embarrassed.

"Yeah. Why don't you go change your shirt, then we'll head over to see Gommy? I'll call Edna to see if she can come by the hospital later on to get you. I may need to stay the night."

"Am I gonna spend the night at her house?" Sam yelled as she ran to her room for a clean shirt.

Sam loved to spend the night with Miss Edna and Mr. Bill. Having them around was like having a full set of grandparents. Spending the night at their house was usually a blast. Miss Edna always baked chocolate chip cookies and, several times, even tried to teach Sam how to make them. Then, there was Mr. Bill. Sometimes he pretended to be a bit grumpy, but Sam knew it was only an act. Annoying Miss Edna was one of his most perfected talents.

"It's just the way we do things 'round here," he'd say. When Sam and Mr. Bill were alone, he was always telling jokes and bragging on his tractor. The only man that she had ever really gotten to know, she liked him a lot.

Laura Lea

"No, she's staying here. No need to pack a bag." Jillian yelled from the kitchen.

"Hey, Mooom," Sam called as she pulled on her denim shirt. "Grab a bag of cheese doodles for me to eat on the way."

Returning to the kitchen, dressed in a cotton shirt covered with flowers, Sam was ready to go.

"Mom, can I take Gommy a gift?"

"I guess that'd be okay," Jillian said as she watched her daughter gallop back down the hallway.

"I'll meet you at the car," Sam yelled disappearing into Gommy's bedroom.

At the sound of the car door opening, Jillian looked up to see her mother's Flower Garden quilt crawling into the car. Filling the front seat, the wadded blob of color fell into a clump revealing a smiling Sam.

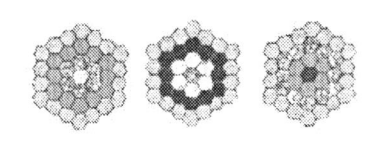

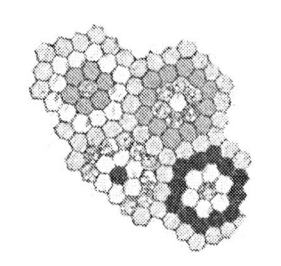

Chapter 14
Fear of the Unknown

During the drive to the hospital, the only sound was crunching as Sam ate her cheese doodles. Neither spoke, as they contemplated the future. While driving down Main Street, Sam noticed dark clouds racing her to the hospital. The sea of blue that hovered overhead earlier in the day was quickly being overrun by an angry gray canopy. If her mom didn't put 'the pedal to the metal', there would be no chance of a trip down victory lane.

Sam didn't like rain, she never had, but today it matched her mood. As she watched the clouds make their final push toward the finish line, large drops of water hit the van's windshield. Random splats fell like tears as the sky began to cry for Gommy.

Realizing that she had been holding her breath, Sam exhaled as they crossed the finish line, the checkered flag marking her arrival. Picking up their pace, the raindrops now slapped the front window of

Cut from the Same Cloth

the van at a steady rate. Sam wanted to focus her thoughts on her grandmother, but the rain begged her for attention, its noisy chatter making it impossible for her to concentrate. Wondering how long the rain would last, she hoped to see the blue skies again very soon.

*　❁　*

During the drive to the hospital, Jillian knew she was witnessing a new side of her daughter, one she had never seen before. Sam was being uncharacteristically quiet. Jillian wondered if her daughter was thinking about their discussion from earlier in the day. Right before her eyes, her daughter was growing up.

Knowing that Sam had always been able to adapt rather quickly didn't prevent Jillian from worrying about how her daughter would handle the hospital and her visit with Gommy. Silently, she promised her daughter that she would not force her to leave Gommy's side until she was ready.

The whole hospital experience was new for Sam. Because of her age, she had never been allowed to enter the ward area. For years, she had complained that the rule banning kids under ten years of age was unfair, so the fact that her first visit was to see her dying grandmother was bittersweet. In the back of her mind, she was starting to think the rule about children visiting the hospital might not be such a bad idea after all. She never in a million years expected to be afraid.

Laura Lea

As they drove, Jillian wondered how she could prepare her daughter for what she would see when they reached Gommy's room.

Gommy was beginning to look pale and the coughing fits had continued to worsen. Unsure of what Sam was expecting, she knew her daughter would be shocked. There were tubes and monitors and bags of fluid hanging from hooks. She couldn't let Sam walk into the room without giving her some idea of what to expect. It would frighten her, Jillian was sure of it.

They parked the car, but neither made any attempt to get out. The rain, that had fallen with such intensity just a few minutes ago, had slowed to a drizzle.

"Mom?" Sam whispered.

"Yes."

"Do you think Gommy would be mad at me if I didn't go in to visit her?"

Sensing an unexpected hesitation, Jillian moved closer to her daughter. Her question came from out of the blue. Only moments earlier, Sam had been thrilled at the prospects of seeing her grandmother.

"What's wrong?" Jillian asked.

"Well, it's not that I don't wanna see Gommy, 'cause I do. It's just that, well, I'm—."

"Scared," Jillian finished, letting Sam off the hook.

"You know what, honey, I'm a little scared, too," Jillian said trying to comfort her daughter.

"Sam, I promise I won't leave you. Listen, if you decide you don't want to go into Gommy's room, I'll see if Nurse Peggy will let you sit with her in the nurse's station while I check on Mom."

Frustrated with herself, Jillian wondered if she was capable of reassuring her daughter. For Sam's whole

Cut from the Same Cloth

life, she had been forced to rely on Gommy for most of her emotional needs. How could Jillian expect her daughter to accept her efforts without reservation? That was unfair to Sam. At this point, however, Jillian had no choice. She had to do what she thought was best for her daughter. It would require patience on her part, and she knew she owed Sam this.

Sensing there were more questions swirling around in Sam's pretty little head, Jillian waited patiently, allowing her daughter time to organize her thoughts. She assumed there was no need to hurry, there had been no call from Dr. Avery to inform her of changes in her mother's condition. It wouldn't hurt to stay in the car for a while, if that would give Sam a chance to talk through what she was feeling. Not easily spooked, Jillian knew her daughter was suffering from the fear of the unknown.

Sam had never been one to shy away from anything. This, however, was different. For the first time in her life, she was drifting in uncharted waters, searching for a beacon to guide her. The one person she could count on was unable to help her, giving her no choice but to trust her mother.

Jillian wanted desperately to make this easier for Sam, but she didn't have the foggiest notion how to go about it. If only Gommy could give her some advice. After all, Gommy knew Sam well. She would know exactly how to handle this.

As they sat silently in the front two seats of the van, Jillian reached her hand over and gently squeezed her daughter's shoulder, hoping the massaging motion would help her to relax.

Embarrassed to ask her next question, Sam turned toward the window before she spoke.

Laura Lea

"Does Gommy look like she's...?" Sam couldn't even force the word from her mouth.

For the first time, Jillian realized Sam's wild imagination must surely be working overtime.

"I'm not sure I understand what you're asking me."

"You know, Mom, does she look like Gommy?

"Of course, she looks like Gommy." Jillian answered. "What were you expecting her to look like?"

"I don't know. I'm not really sure."

"Hmm." Jillian mused, her index finger propped against the corner of her mouth.

"Well, she hasn't had a shower in a week, the back of her hair is flat. Uh...and she's not wearing lipstick. Other than that she looks like Gommy. Oh, and she's a little pale, but not too bad. Now that I think about it, that doesn't really sound like Gommy at all, does it?"

Pausing to give Sam's mind time to paint a mental picture, Jillian finally spoke.

"Hey, Sam, don't mention anything to Gommy about her hair, okay? You know how it bothers her when her hair and makeup aren't perfect." Jillian smiled hoping a little humor would help ease Sam's nervous jitters.

"You know, Sam, Gommy's pretty weak, and she's still coughing a lot. I think it's getting harder for her to breathe, too."

"Will she know who I am?" Sam asked, her eyes looking sadder with each passing minute.

"Will she know who you are? What kind of question is that?" Jillian teased.

"Her eyesight's the same as it's always been. She's only been gone for a week, I'm sure she hasn't

Cut from the Same Cloth

forgotten you, especially if you blow that cheese doodle breath in her face."

"Do you think she'll want to talk to me?" Sam asked.

"Of course, she will, if she's awake. She was asleep a good bit of the morning, but I got to talk to her just before I left to go home. Don't forget, honey, it's hard for her to talk. The pneumonia's gotten worse, so they're forcing oxygen into her nose to make it easier for her to breathe. You'll see when we get there, she's got a tube taped to her nose. It's giving her more—."

"She's got a tube in her nose?" Sam questioned.

"Uh-huh, her lungs aren't working like they should be. The tube helps her out a little. Hopefully, she can breathe easier."

"Mom, does it hurt when you can't get enough oxygen?" Sam asked with a pained look on her face.

"I don't think it hurts very much. I think it just makes you panic. It's sort of like trying to breath with your nose pinched and your hand over your mouth," Jillian explained.

Wanting to understand just how her grandmother was feeling, Sam reached up with her right hand and pinched her nose, with her left hand she covered her mouth. Trying to breath, she was amazed at how tiring her experiment was.

Jillian smiled at her daughter, wondering exactly what she was thinking as she tried to simulate her grandmother's present circumstances.

Poor Gommy, she thought.

"I hope she's awake. I can't wait to see her face when she sees you standing beside her bed," Jillian said. "It's gonna make her day. Ya know, Sam, she's been asking for you."

"For me?" Sam looked surprised.

Laura Lea

"Yeah, I think she's missed you most of all."

"I've missed her, too...a lot," Sam whispered, her mind already somewhere else.

"She's got something she wants to tell you."

Ignoring what her mother had just said, Sam spoke up, her eyes beginning to tear again.

"Mom, do you think Gommy's really gonna die?"

Out of habit, she grabbed the corner of her shirt and began to dry her eyes, but with the nose yuck incident still fresh in her mind, she quickly dropped it, deciding to use her fingers instead.

"Well, I guess I'm ready to go now," Sam said reaching for her grandmother's quilt that was wadded up in the rear floorboard of her mother's van.

Suddenly, turning back toward her mother with both arms outstretched, she dropped the quilt, then grabbed her mother's neck so tightly Jillian could barely breathe.

Maybe it's too soon, Jillian thought. *Maybe Sam is too young to see someone like this. Is she trying to tell me she doesn't want to go in?*

For that matter, Jillian wasn't sure she was ready to go in, either. Wishing she knew how to read her daughter better, Jillian's heart began to ache for what Sam was soon going to experience. Maybe it was a good thing that children were kept from going into the patient's rooms. Sam wouldn't even be here if Dr. Avery hadn't suggested it.

Calm for the moment, her arms wrapped around her mother's neck, Sam thought of her mother and of Gommy. They were really the only two people she had as far as family went. Even though she wasn't as close to her mother as she was to her grandmother, she still loved her. There was, also, Mr. Bill and Miss Edna, whom she had always considered to be an

Cut from the Same Cloth

adopted set of grandparents. She also had her best friend, Mickey, but he wasn't family.

To Sam, the thought of losing her grandmother was unimaginable. As far back as she could remember, Gommy was practically front and center in every memory. How would she bear a life without her? If Gommy's doctor was right, Sam might very well lose her grandmother and her dearest friend, all at the same time.

Was it possible to have a broken heart? If so, Sam was sure hers was, at the very least, cracked. She closed her eyes, and while her mother softly stroked her hair, she tried to remember the last time she and her grandmother had been together before Dr. Avery admitted her to the hospital.

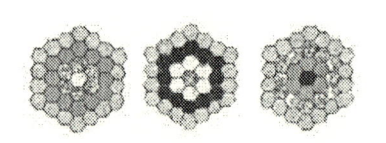

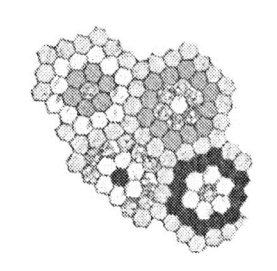

Chapter 15
History Lesson

Thursday Night

  Sam was almost positive she and Gommy had spent last Thursday night together. She didn't recall her mother being at home, and the only night of the week that she was ever gone was Thursday. Sure that she was right, she remembered her mother waltzing in the kitchen door, proudly displaying a yellow layer cake covered with butter cream roses that she had decorated during a class at the local bakery.
  "Check it out," she had said, beaming as she cut each of them a huge slice covered with pink roses.
  Gommy wasn't feeling well that night, so Sam prepared their supper. Wearing her grandmother's favorite print apron and an elastic bowl cover for a hair net, she was the perfect chef. Gathering the ingredients from the pantry, she prepared a feast for the two of them to share. Rather than have Gommy

Cut from the Same Cloth

come to the kitchen, Sam decided to carry the 'fruits of her labor' to her grandmother.

Making her entrance into the bedroom, backside first, she bumped the door open with her bottom, spun around on her heel, displaying a shiny metal cookie sheet containing a plate mounded with food, a small bud vase containing a paper mache peony, and two green bottled colas.

Together, they shared saltine crackers, smeared with peanut butter, green grapes, and cheese doodles. As far as Sam was concerned, the meal was worthy of five stars, but Gommy had been unable to eat, barely taking enough bites to down a single cracker.

❋✪❋

*A*fter dinner, Sam cleared away the tray and joined Gommy under her quilt.

"Gommy, will you tell me some more about your quilt?" Sam asked.

"I s'pose I could, but just for a little while, okay? Anything in particular you want to know?"

"Well," she said, her eyes marveling at the tiny stitches that held together the old fabric. "See that torn spot in the corner? What is that white stuff that's hanging out?" Sam said pointing to the corner hexagon that was worn thin revealing the remains of the original cotton ball batting.

"Oh, that there's the batting. Back when I was a girl, our neighbors grew cotton for the cotton mill here in town. Do you remember hearing me talk about the mill?"

"Yes, ma'am."

Laura Lea

"That's where I met Rose and Daisy and Fern."
"What about Miss Iris?" Sam quizzed. "Didn't she work there, too? And, hey, isn't that where you met my granddaddy?"
"Well, Iris is Fern's first cousin, that's how we met. And I met your granddaddy at chur...."
Catching herself in mid-sentence, she realized that she was about to open a can of worms that she really wasn't up to dealing with.
"But I thought he worked at the mill."
Sam hopped out of the bed, ran toward the curio cabinet, grabbed a small heart-shaped pewter picture frame from the shelf, then leaped back onto the bed.
"Is this him?" she asked handing the frame to her grandmother.
Holding the photograph close, Gommy gazed at the creased black and white picture of a handsome gentleman wearing black slacks and a solid black minister's shirt for several minutes, finally looking away. Washed over by a wave of sudden memories, she was lost somewhere in time.
"Hey, Gommy," Sam said, pulling on her grandmother's arm. "Did you hear me?"
"No, I"m sorry, what did you say?"
"Is this my granddaddy?"
Laying the frame down on the bedside table, Gommy rejoined her granddaughter in conversation.
"I thought you wanted me to tell you about the quilt batting. When I was young, Daddy used to do odd jobs for our neighbors, and sometimes they'd pay him in cotton. Momma would spread the cotton out on the quilt back, then she'd start her quilting.
"Good Lord, child, I guess we'd have froze to death in the winter, if it wasn't for those cotton stuffed quilts."

Cut from the Same Cloth

"This one sure is warm," Sam said snuggling closer to her grandmother. "Hey, Gommy, I wonder how many stitches there are in this quilt."

"Haven't the foggiest idea, but I know that every one of 'em was stitched with love. Just knowin' that's always made it feel a little bit warmer.

"When I was younger and still living with Aunt Sophia, I used to wrap myself up in this quilt at night and pretend I was back home, snuggled all warm and cozy in my own bed. Felt like I was gettin' a great big hug," Gommy said, staring into space.

"This quilt's got so many stories, I bet it's a hundred years old," Sam wagered.

"A hundred years old? I beg your pardon, I do not look a hundred years old. Don't forget this started out as my baby quilt."

"So that makes it sixty...."

"Seven. That's right, I'm sixty-seven years old. So that makes this quilt right at sixty-seven, too. My lands, this quilt's been with me for a long time. It's in pretty good shape to be that old, even if I do say so myself. Of course, I didn't use it all sixty-seven of those years. I kept it in my hope chest for a long time, well, up until I moved in here after your da...." Gommy paused unsure if she should continue.

"After what, Gommy?" Sam begged, tugging on her grandmother's gown.

"After your daddy died," she said, her eyes smiling with compassion.

Sam loved to hear stories about her father. He died when she was two, and she couldn't remember anything about him. Gommy usually didn't mind telling her about her father, but her mother, well, that was a different story. Even though, there were pictures of him in her mother's bedroom, her mother

Laura Lea

never wanted to talk about him. It had occurred to Sam on several occasions that her mother might be trying to forget him all together.

Interrupting Sam's thoughts, Gommy continued on, "This quilt's pretty worn, but I wouldn't take anything for it. Maybe one day, I'll leave it to you."

"What did you say?" Sam asked, having never heard that phrase before.

"The quilt. honey, would you like to have it after I die? I won't be needin' it then. So I thought I might leave it to you, if you'd like to have it."

"But, Gommy, I don't want you to die just so I can have your quilt. I can sit under it any time I want, right?"

Seeing the look of panic on Sam's face, once again Gommy decided to change the subject.

"Did I ever tell you what the name of this quilt pattern is?"

"Grandma's Flower Garden," Sam said in a disgusted tone, wanting to hear more about her father. "But why do you call it that?"

Pointing to the yellow hexagons, Gommy went on to explain how the fabrics were joined together, each having a center of yellow, the finished quilt resembling a flower garden.

For a moment, the two of them sat together in silence, both examining the flowers on Gommy's quilt. Sam wondering when and where each fabric was worn, and Gommy remembering the pieces of her past that had found their way into her granddaughter's future.

"Were you scared when you left home?" Sam asked softly.

135

Cut from the Same Cloth

"No, not really. I was nineteen, almost twenty. I guess it was probably time for me to grow up anyway, you know, move on. Moving to a new place isn't always sad or scary. Sometimes, people move because it's the best thing to do. After I came to live in the city I missed my momma and daddy, but they really needed some extra money, and since I was the oldest, I was the only one who could help. I wasn't all that anxious to leave home, but I did it 'cause I knew I should.

"Of course, I was lucky that Aunt Sophia was able to get me on at the cotton mill. I worked with her in the office as a file clerk. Every week, I'd send half my paycheck home to Momma. I did that for years, until I lost my job when the mill closed down. Sometimes I'd get lonely, but it really wasn't so bad here.

"I stayed fairly busy during the day. There just wasn't a whole lot of time to think much about missin' home. It was after supper when I'd get homesick. Most nights, I'd just go to my room and go on to bed. I read a lot of books back then. Once or twice a week, I'd write a letter to Momma. That was it.

"I guess I'd been here about three months when I met Rose and Daisy, then a little later, Fern and Iris. We'd go out dancing on the weekends or go to the movie. We used to have a big time, but even then, I still couldn't wait to get home so I could crawl into bed, wrap this quilt around me and dream of home.

"Yes, siree, this here's a special quilt, Samantha Louise, and I'd love for you to have it one day. Of course, you'd have to promise me that you'd try to remember all of the stories I've told you about this quilt. You know, Sam, you're the only one who knows'em. You can be the keeper of the quilt."

Laura Lea

"Huh?"

"You know, like the keeper of the flame."

That was the last thing of importance that her grandmother said to her. Gommy slept in the following morning, and by the time, Sam returned home from school that day, she was already in the hospital.

❀ ✿ ❀

While sitting in the van, her head resting on her mother's shoulder, her grandmother's quilt resting on her lap, Sam realized that it was Friday. Gommy had been in the hospital for an entire week, but to Sam, it seemed like a lot longer.

Had Gommy suspected last Thursday night she might die? It wasn't like her to talk about giving away her quilt. After all, it was her most prized possession.

Sam had been still for so long, Jillian wondered if her daughter had fallen asleep exhausted from the emotional afternoon. Gently, she shook her daughter.

"Sam, you asleep?"

"No, I was just thinking about something Gommy told me."

"Wanna tell me about it?" Jillian asked.

"Oh, you know, the story about her Flower Garden quilt."

Sam would have been content to sit there for a while longer, but it was obvious her mother was anxious to get inside. Jillian had taken a tube of lipstick from her black leather shoulder bag and begun to reapply it for the umpteenth time.

Cut from the Same Cloth

Watching her mother smear Crushed Petals lipstick on her lips, Sam couldn't help but grin at the face her mother made when her lips slid past each other. After returning the tube back to her bag, she pulled out her pocket-size round brush and fluffed her sagging curls.

"I'll be glad when all this rain ends. I'm tired of my hair looking like I stuck a wet finger in a wall outlet," Jillian mumbled.

Throwing the brush back into her bag, she examined herself in the mirror. Pinching both of her cheeks to add some color, she smiled really big into the rearview mirror to inspect her teeth.

Watching this entire set of maneuvers, Sam tried to decide if her mother looked young for someone thirty-seven years old. It was hard to tell, she did have strands of gray in every curl, and small lines just below the outer corners of each eye, but she was still pretty. For the first time in Sam's life, she realized how much her mother resembled her grandmother.

They were a lot alike. For one thing, they both were obsessed with lipstick and hair. They both had greenish-blue eyes and thin noses that turned up slightly at the tip. Except for their hair, Sam suspected her mother would age to look just like Gommy.

"Look, Sam, it's beginning to rain again. Let's get inside before it starts pouring." Jillian said, opening the door to her van. No sooner had Sam looked up than she saw her mother leap over a small puddle only to land right in the middle of a larger one.

"Oh, well," Sam said, opening her door.

Using both hands, she hoisted Gommy's quilt out of the van, hugging it close to keep from dropping it in the wet, dirty parking lot.

Laura Lea

Hearing the sound of the gun blast, she shot from her starting position, running with all of her might. Approaching each hurdle, her short legs kicked their way over the obstacles that lay between her and the hospital's main entrance.

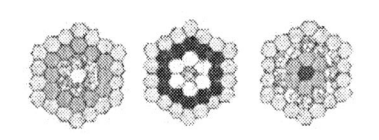

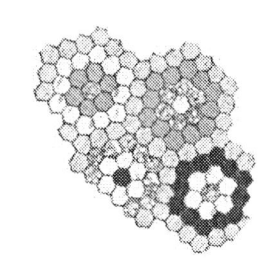

Chapter 16
The Hospital, At Last

Approaching the hospital's original entrance, Sam remembered seeing it every day from the inside of a school bus. Its tall spires and large wooden doors made it look medieval. To Sam, it was the city's lone castle.

Rather than a wall and a moat, it was surrounded by rows of parked cars and concrete. Side by side, they were enemy soldiers attempting to overtake the fortress, claiming it for their own. Sam knew they would never take the castle. After all, no one ever had. Even after all of these years, it still stood as a beacon of strength in their city.

Hoping to enter the castle through the oversized wooden doors, her highness was disappointed to find the main entrance had been moved to the newly built wing. The only people allowed through the wooden doors were the lowly servants.

Cut from the Same Cloth

Disappointed with how everything was working out, Sam followed her mother through the tinted, sliding glass doors.

❖ ❖ ❖

*I*nside the light was blinding. Bouncing from solid white walls onto gleaming white floors, the brilliant light reflected right into Sam's eyes. Amazed by how shiny everything was, she wondered if Mr. Clean was on the payroll. Following her mother down the long hallway, she could hear their shoes strike the floor.

As they made their way deeper into the bowels of the hospital, Sam accidentally squeaked her shoes on the spotless floor, breaking the eerie silence. Two gentlemen dressed in green from head to toe, broke away from their deep conversation to hurl glaring daggers in her direction. As she continued to follow her mother down the quiet hallway, her shoes squealed yet again. This time, however, the gentlemen didn't even acknowledge the interruption. Sam couldn't help herself, she had to do it. So once again, her happy feet squealed with delight.

"Shhh, Sam, don't do that," her mother whispered grabbing her by the hand pulling her down the hall. "Sam, hospitals have rules about that kind of stuff. You *have* to be quiet so that you don't disturb people who are ill."

Speaking loudly to her mother, she asked, "What did I do?"

"Shhhh," Jillian hissed, her right index finger pressed onto her pursed lips. "You have to be quiet in here. So whisper, please!"

Laura Lea

"Why do I have to whisper?" Sam whispered re-adjusting the mounds of fabric that her tiny arms were still holding. "It's not like we're in the library."
Sam didn't think she was going to like this whole hospital thing. She decided she was glad that a silly old rule had kept her out as long as it had. Any minute, she expected to see a gray-haired lady, wearing small reading glasses, jump out at her from behind a door, sounding suspiciously like a tea kettle letting off steam.
Even though Sam had no idea what to expect, she never dreamed it would be so unfriendly.
Startling her, the intercom crackled to life.
"Dr. Hill, report to the O.R. STAT."
Sam was amazed at how the sound seemed to fill the hallway, following them as they made their way to Room 117.
"Here's the nurse's station," Jillian announced as they rounded the corner. "I'll let them know we're here and see how Mom's doing," Jillian said, heading for the desk, but Sam didn't follow.
"Mom, I'll wait out here, okay?"
"I'll only be a minute. You stay right here. I'll just be on the other side of that window," Jillian said, pointing toward the glass wall.
"Yes, ma'am."
With that, Jillian entered the nurse's station. Sam could see her mother as she talked to a short, pudgy lady wearing a pinkish colored nurse's outfit that seemed a bit too small. She couldn't hear their conversation, but the short lady was doing a lot of talking. Before she knew it, her mother and the nurse were walking toward her.
"Sam, this is Nurse LaSauw. She's Gommy's nurse during the daytime.

Cut from the Same Cloth

"Hey there, sugar. Aren't you the cutest thing? We don't get many kids up here on the floor, you know, on account of the rule an' all. So this is a real treat. Now listen, I don't want you to call me Nurse LaSauw, my name's Peggy. Everybody just calls me Peggy or Nurse Peggy, that is, if your momma don't mind. Say what's that you're carrying?"

Sam looked in her mother's direction, her eyes asking to be bailed out.

"Oh," said Jillian. "Well, Sam decided that Mom might get a little cold in her hospital room, so she wanted to bring Mom's favorite quilt to her."

"Well, I'll just be. Aren't you the thoughtful one? Your grandmother's been right about you. Been bragging on you every chance she gets."

Sam was embarrassed at the attention focused on her and quickly ducked her head.

"Thank you, Peggy," Jillian chimed cutting her eyes toward Sam as she waited to hear her daughter say the same thing.

"Thank you, Nurse La...I mean Nurse Peggy," Sam beamed.

"I guess we'll head on to Mom's room now. Let's go, Sam, honey," Jillian said taking her daughter by the arm and gently guiding her to Gommy's room.

Boy, Sam couldn't help but marvel at how grown up she felt. Not only was she in a part of the hospital that was typically off limits, but she was also getting to call an adult by her first name.

"I'm awful glad Dr. Avery let you come up to visit. Your momma tells me this is your first trip to the hospital. And you brought a special gift for your grandmother. Why, isn't that the prettiest old quilt I've ever seen?

Laura Lea

"Jillian, my shift ends at seven, so I'll be here a little while longer. The last time I checked on your mother, she was asleep, but she may be awake by now. Why don't the two of you go on in and visit with her for a little while? I'll try to come by after I finish making my rounds."

Sam had never heard anybody spit so many words out so quickly.

Somebody should tell her that she needs to take a breath while she's talking, or she might turn blue and pass out, Sam thought.

It was obvious that Nurse Peggy loved to talk, and she seemed like a really happy person, too. Her whole body seemed to smile when she walked. As Nurse Peggy turned to leave, Sam noticed how quickly her short legs strutted down the hallway. Grinning to herself, Sam couldn't help but notice how much her new friend reminded her of Petunia, Mr. Bill's momma pig.

❋ ✿ ❋

Jillian took Sam by the hand and led her to Gommy's room.

"This way, Sam."

When they reached the door, Sam was surprised to see her grandmother's name printed on the nameplate beside the door.

    BLACK, LOUISE P.
    #67109
    DR. S. AVERY.

Cut from the Same Cloth

She had always been proud of the fact that she was named for her grandmother, but at the same time, if she was really honest, she was glad that everybody called her Sam and not Louise. Louise was a lovely name for a grandmother, but it seemed a little floral for a kid like Sam.

Jillian headed in through the door, but Sam stopped short.

"What's wrong, honey?" Jillian asked.

"Mom, I don't...."

"It's okay, Sam. I'll be here. Come on in, let's see if Mom's awake." Jillian reached out, taking Sam's hand and pulled her into the room.

Sam was a little hesitant at first, drawing back slightly on her mother's hand. Entering the room, she was struck by the contrast. The hallway had been brightly lit, almost cheerful, but Gommy's room was quite the opposite. The curtains were closed, and the only light in the room was coming from a long rectangular box on the wall behind the bed. It was very dreary.

She was unable to see clearly in the dimly lit room, but her ability to feel was working just fine. The room was so warm. Sam thought she might suffocate and yet, she felt chilled. Crossing her arms, she tried to warm herself.

After her eyes adjusted to the lighting, she could see the room that had been her grandmother's home for almost a week. It didn't even seem real. Sam could hear her mother's voice as she greeted her grandmother. Wanting to do the same, Sam turned to see a stranger lying in the hospital bed.

"Good afternoon, sleepy head. I brought someone to see you. Guess who? I brought Sam," Jillian teased cheerfully, watching for a response from her mother.

Laura Lea

Moving closer to the bed, Jillian couldn't help but notice how rosy her mother's cheeks were compared to her earlier visit this morning. If she hadn't known better, she would have sworn her mother had just come in from her garden. At the bedside, she leaned in close to give her mother a kiss on the forehead and stopped short keenly aware that a halo of heat was radiating from her mother's ailing form.
It is a little warm in here, she thought. *Surely that's not the reason for her color.*
Placing her hand on her mother's forehead, it was obvious that the fever was back with a vengeance. Not wanting to alarm Gommy or Sam, Jillian spoke quietly.
"Mom, I think you might have a little bit of fever. I'll go find Peggy and see if she can give you some medicine for it."
Turning to leave, she stopped suddenly.
Where's Sam? she wondered.
Having been preoccupied with her mother, she had almost forgotten that Sam was with her. Turning to find her daughter, the moment she saw Sam's face, it was clear that she was frightened. Jillian had tried to prepare her daughter, but clearly she had failed. Everything about the room and her grandmother had taken Sam by surprise. With her eyes wide, she stood perfectly still, arms crossed at her chest, as if she knew a hug might somehow make this easier.
Reaching out to hold Sam's hand, Jillian spoke, "Sam, you alright?"
"Uh-huh," she said quietly.
"I need to find Nurse Peggy, I think Mom's got a fever. Will you be alright if I leave just long enough to find her? It shouldn't take but a minute."

Cut from the Same Cloth

While Jillian clearly heard the word *yes* come from Sam's mouth, her daughter's eyes were screaming *NO*.

"I can wait here for you," Sam said with some hesitation. "Just hurry back, okay?"

As Jillian left the room, she fought to control her emotions.

Poor Sam, I hate it that you had to see Gommy like this. There just wasn't any other way.

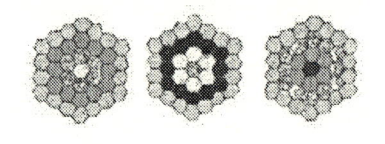

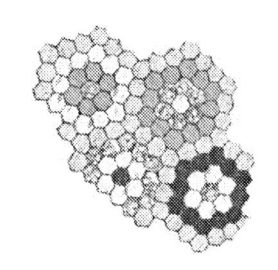

Chapter 17
Saying Goodbye

With Jillian gone, Sam was alone with her grandmother. She took a minute to scan the small, pale blue room. It was excruciatingly plain.

She allowed her eyes to rest on the woman lying in the hospital bed. It couldn't be her grandmother. Just last week, Gommy had been sick, but she still looked fairly healthy. Now her hair was mashed into several flips and humps, and her lips were dry and cracked.

Poor Gommy, she thought. *She'd just die if anyone saw her like this.* It broke Sam's heart to know that her grandmother had no control over any of this. None of them did.

Unable to look at Gommy any longer, her eyes flitted around the dimly lit room. Taking her time, she studied each one of the machines and gadgets that were no doubt helping her grandmother stay alive.

Why did she suddenly feel queasy?

Cut from the Same Cloth

Countless nights, she and Gommy had spent the entire evening glued to the television, a bag of microwave popcorn propped between them, watching a medical procedure being performed for the television audience. Never before had any of the procedures or equipment made her tummy feel the slightest bit bubbly.

Now, however, she was frantically exploring her options for getting as much fresh air as possible. Short of borrowing Gommy's air hose, she had no options. Summoning all of her concentration, she focused her attention on each item trying to determine its use.

Never before had Sam seen anyone she knew hooked up to so many different things. There was a bag of clear liquid hanging from the pole that stood beside the bed. From the bag, a steady drip continued to flow through a clear tube that was taped to the back of Gommy's wrist. Another tube ran into her nose and was held in place by a wide piece of flesh-colored tape. From her grandmother's nose, she let her eyes follow the tubing down to the floor and then back up to a rectangular object that looked similar to a temperature gauge mounted on the wall behind the bed. Attached to the gauge, a bottle of clear liquid bubbled continuously.

On the other side of the bed stood a blue machine that displayed blinking red numbers. Sam had no idea what any of the numbers meant, but their steady flickering seemed to have a hypnotizing effect.

Ashamed to admit that she was avoiding her grandmother's bed, Sam wondered what Gommy must be thinking of her.

All week long, Sam had been a piece of driftwood floating along in the sea wondering when she might wash ashore. Isolated and alone, she'd wondered if

Laura Lea

she would ever feel solid ground beneath her feet again. As she stood in the room with her grandmother, she expected to feel safe, but she didn't. Unable to really say how she was feeling, she knew only one thing for sure. Her grandmother didn't look well, not very well at all.

There were so many things that Sam had planned on telling Gommy when she finally got to see her again. There was the letter from Mickey Sullivan, and the funny story of how she killed the large monster with her pencil. Yet, for some reason, they no longer seemed important.

All week long, she had complained profusely to her mother about the rule that prevented children under ten from being allowed on the patient floors of the hospital. Now that she was here, she understood why. All she really wanted to do was go home. Never in a million years had she expected any of this. Gommy had been in the hospital several times before, but she had always come home. Sam had assumed that this time would be no different.

It was then that Sam heard her grandmother's voice. It was soft, hoarse, and yet still sweetly familiar. Having been standing still for so long, Sam had forgotten that she was holding her grandmother's quilt.

"Sammy," Gommy whispered, "don't be afraid." Gommy had called her by their special nickname.

Drawn to her grandmother's bedside, Sam slowly walked toward the bed, allowing her eyes to rest on her grandmother's face.

"Gommy,...I brought you your quilt. I thought you might be cold."

Cut from the Same Cloth

There, smiling up from a body that Sam barely recognized, were the kindest eyes she had ever known.

"Bless you, child."

Spreading it over the bed, she smoothed the wrinkles with her hands. Forgetting her fear, Sam took her grandmother's hand in her own. If she hadn't seen it for herself, she would have sworn she was holding the roots of a small tree. Never before had she noticed how knotted and twisted her grandmother's fingers were. Now, they were so puffy, too. Was this what arthritis did to people? Had being in the hospital made it worse?

Her mother was right, Gommy was warm. Gazing at her grandmother, Sam noticed Gommy's paper thin skin and bluish veins.

Oh Gommy, she thought *what have they done to you? What's happening to you?*

"Gommy," Sam whispered as she bent to kiss her grandmother's warm cheek. "I missed you."

Without warning, Gommy's frail body raised up in a coughing fit. Nurse Sam reacted, placing her hand behind her grandmother's back to support her until the fit ended. The coughing spell over, Sam gently eased her grandmother back onto her pillow. The crud still clung stubbornly to the walls of her infected lungs.

Even with all of her hacking, the clumps of yucky grey-green mucus refused to budge, content to rattle around inside her chest like a ghost in a haunted house. Sam wished there was some way she could help Gommy get rid of all of the junk in her lungs and throat, but she was all out of ideas.

Realizing that the coughing had taken all of Gommy's strength, Sam was amazed at how lifeless

Laura Lea

her grandmother was. If it hadn't been for the labored breathing, it would have been easy to assume that she was already dead. Watching Gommy's chest rise and fall, it was clearly a struggle for her to breathe.

Sam knew it was rude to stare, but she couldn't help it.

How did Gommy get in such pitiful shape? she wondered.

If Gommy could see herself, she would be yelling for someone to get a hairdresser to her room S.T.A.T. Not one to be slack with her appearance, her hair and makeup were always perfect. Now that Sam thought about it, she couldn't remember ever seeing her grandmother leave their house with her hair unpinned, and her face unmade.

"I never know when I might see someone I know," she always said with a chuckle. "I wouldn't want to embarrass you, my dear."

"Gommy, would like for me to put some of Mom's lipstick on your lips?" Sam asked, knowing it would no doubt make her feel better.

Opening her eyes, she smiled and nodded.

"I'll get Mom's purse. I know she's got some in there."

Reaching for her mother's purse, Sam continued to talk, "I'll put some lip balm on them first."

Cramming her fingers into the front pocket of her blue jeans, she pulled out a flavored lip balm.

"Gee, Gommy, I'm sorry. All I have is one that tastes like chocolate chip cookie dough. Is that alright?"

Seeing her grandmother smile, she removed the top from the tube and gently slid the soothing balm back and forth across Gommy's dry, cracked lips. As Gommy wiggled her lips pressing them together, the scent of freshly baked cookies floated toward Sam.

Cut from the Same Cloth

"Feels better," she whispered.

"Oh, I'm not done." Holding her mother's lipstick in front of Gommy, Sam waved it back and forth to show her grandmother the color.

"Hey, Goms, you're in luck. Mom's got your favorite shade, Crushed Petals."

Sam applied the lipstick carefully trying not to smear it on the wrinkled skin that met creased edges of her grandmother's lips. Gommy despised it when her lipstick used her wrinkles as a way to migrate to the other sections of her face.

"Now, you look just like my grandmother! Feel better?"

"Better," Gommy whispered trying hard to catch her breath.

"Would you like for me to brush your hair? I'll be careful."

The frail head nodded yes. Sam wasn't sure if Gommy really wanted her to, but playing beauty parlor was something they did all the time.

"Where's your brush?"

Sam knew that Gommy would have her special brush with her. It was one of her most beloved possessions. Motioning to the drawer in the bedside table, Gommy tried to sit up and get it herself.

"I'll get it, Gommy," Sam said working her way around the bed to the table.

Opening the drawer, she found the sterling silver hairbrush. It was an heirloom that she had been given before Jillian was born. Sam never understood why Gommy loved it so much, especially since it had someone else's initials on it.

Unlike any brush Sam had ever seen, its mirrored backside was beautifully engraved with a swirly heart that held the letters, L. P. C. Amazed that her

Laura Lea

grandmother had been able to keep up with a hairbrush for all those years, Sam admired its beauty. With her fingers, she felt its cool, smooth surface.

Gently, she brushed her grandmother's hair, working to smooth down the sections that were mashed into humps on the sides of her head.

"Gommy, you look beautiful. I wish I had a mirror so you—."

No sooner had the words left her mouth, than she realized that she could use the backside of the hairbrush. It wouldn't be perfect, but it would be better than nothing at all. Using the hem of her shirt she shined the engraved side of the hairbrush.

"Here you go."

Holding the brush up so that Gommy could see herself in its mirrored back, she held it close, hoping Gommy could get a glimpse of her hair and lips.

Without warning, tears began to fall from her grandmother's eyes. With Gommy's gnarled finger, she traced the letters engraved on the brush.

Why is she doing this? Sam wondered, hoping she had not hurt her grandmother's feelings.

"I'm sorry, I didn't mean to hurt your feelings," Sam whispered, as Gommy patted her hand.

Suddenly, another fit of coughing started. This time, Gommy rolled onto her side facing away from Sam. That's when the bag of yellow liquid became visible. There was no need to ask what the bag held. Sam knew exactly what it was.

After Gommy's surgery last year, her grandmother had been forced to carry around a bag for her urine for several days. Sam remembered how embarrassed her grandmother had been.

Oh, Gommy, she thought, *look at you.* With that Sam could no longer contain her sadness. Being brave for

Cut from the Same Cloth

her grandmother's sake was far too difficult. It was no longer possible to pretend.

❀ ✿ ❀

After leaving the nurse's station, Jillian made her way to the room. Entering, she saw the tears spilling from her daughter's eyes. When she saw Sam's head resting on her mother's pillow, the Flower Garden quilt spread neatly over the bed, she, too, wanted to cry. Backing up towards the door, she decided to give the two of them a little more time alone. Jillian knew she would never forget the tender moment she had just witnessed. There, in front of her, were the two people she loved most in the world, saying goodbye in their own way.

Jillian was grateful that Sam had gotten to visit with her grandmother one last time. While Jillian's head told her to leave the room, that she was eavesdropping on a private moment, her heart begged her to stay.

She considered it a privilege to be witnessing one of life's most misunderstood mysteries: the passing of a life. She felt both humbled and honored to be with her mother during her last precious moments. Jillian would be there to see her mother's mystery unfold.

The first time, she experienced the death of a loved one, Jillian had not really cared. Her father had died when she was twenty-three. They had not seen each other in years, and their only communication had been cards with money at different times of the year.

Laura Lea

Then, there was Peter's death. It had taken her by surprise. Tragically, she had never gotten to tell him goodbye. Now, she would be forced to face death again. This time, however, God had been generous allowing her the opportunity to tell her mother goodbye.

Jillian was struck by how totally different Peter's death was compared to her mother's. Yet, in the end, both scenes would produce the same outcome for the main character. In some ways, it was comforting to know that this time she knew what was coming. There would be no sudden surprises. This time she would say goodbye.

Jillian realized that her mother was passing the torch. Gommy had carried it proudly for seven years, tenderly guarding Sam's heart, but the time had come to let Jillian have her second chance.

Not wanting to interfere as her mother and her daughter said what could possibly be their final goodbye, Jillian quietly remained at the door.

❖ ◉ ❖

"Oh, Gommy, I am afraid," Sam cried. "What'll I do without you? Please, don't leave me. I won't have anybody if you go."

As Jillian watched and listened from the dark shadow by the door, her daughter's words were daggers plunged deeply into her heart. It was the first time she had ever heard Sam express her true feelings about their relationship. Sadly, she wasn't surprised.

Who could blame Sam for being attached to her grandmother? If she was truly honest with herself,

Cut from the Same Cloth

Jillian knew it was Sam who should be the object of her pity, not herself. After all, she was the adult.

With her mother slipping away, there was no choice. She had to put the past behind her for Sam's sake, and move on.

As she watched the tender moment, she realized how precious the passage of time was. Just a few feet away was her past and her future. It was true what they say about 'time healing all hurts'. Even now, with the ticking of the clock, the passage of time was washing away old hurts to reveal the hope that every tomorrow brings.

Tomorrow would be a new day, one to embrace with all it chose to offer. Jillian could feel deeply within her soul that this night would bring deep sorrow, yet she felt a calming reassurance that when the sun rose tomorrow morning, she would have a chance to try again, the elusive second chance. This time she would face the new day with hope.

As if the lights of her soul had been turned on, she realized for the first time just how much her mother had done for her.

Selflessly, Gommy had given up her retirement years to help raise her grandchild. Even in her death, she was teaching her daughter how to be a better mother. Hoping she had paid close enough attention, Jillian prayed that her own daughter would give her a second chance.

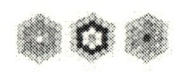

❋ ✪ ❋

Startled by the commotion at her mother's bed, Jillian looked up to see Sam climb onto the bed and

Laura Lea

crawl under the quilt. Stretching out beside her grandmother, she began to weep.

At first Sam cried quietly, keeping her emotions in check, but eventually, she lost control, her sobbing impossible to ignore.

Realizing that Sam needed to be comforted, Jillian rushed to the bedside where she put her arms around her grief stricken child.

Sam turned toward her mother. Their tear-filled eyes locked, giving each of them the courage to embrace. As they held each other tightly, Sam could feel their hearts beating as if they were sounding out a battle cry.

For the first time, it seemed the battle was over. Unable to control herself any longer, words began to pour from Jillian's mouth as if she were trying to beat a clock.

"Oh, Mom, how can I ever thank you? You kept my baby for me all these years. I'm okay now. I can do this. I want to take care of Sam. I'm not afraid."

Jillian could feel her mother's grip as it tightened around her arm. She bent to listen as Gommy fought to breathe and speak at the same time. Jillian knew it would be the last time she would hear her mother's voice.

"I'd do it...again...proud of you. Take her home... going, too...bottom drawer...love you, Jilly."

"I love you, too, Mom. Goodbye."

Except for the sound of Gommy's shallow breaths and the hum of the machines, the room was peacefully quiet. Snuggled under Gommy's quilt, three generations of women held onto each other. They shed tears of sorrow and joy. Each one hopeful about the future and at peace with the past.

Cut from the Same Cloth

After a while, Gommy squeezed both of their hands and turned toward Jillian.

"Take Sammy home," she whispered so softly that Jillian wasn't sure if she actually heard her mother or just read her lips.

Jillian had planned to stay the night, but she knew there was no point in arguing with her mother. They had already said goodbye. If she and Sam left now, they could let Gommy die with dignity. Even in death, her mother was trying to shelter her. Jillian knew that Gommy would not want them to see her die. To leave now would be best for everyone.

Once again, her mother was right. Even though it would break her heart to leave her mother's side, she would do it as a final gesture of gratitude for all that her mother had done for her.

Kissing Gommy goodbye one last time, she gathered her mother's things from the bedside cabinet, tucked her mother in tightly under her quilt, and took Sam home.

Four hours later, Louise Black went home, too.

❀✪❀

*I*t had been a long day, and all Sam wanted to do was go to bed. She kissed her mother goodnight and went to her room. Most nights, Sam would read herself to sleep, but tonight she wasn't in the mood.

After crawling into bed, she turned off the light and watched a sea of twinkling stars dance across her ceiling. The whole star thing had been Gommy's idea.

Sam could not help but smile as she recalled the night the stars were placed on the ceiling. Even in the

Laura Lea

pitch black room, she could see her grandmother teetering on the top of an old step ladder. With her arms stretched high above her head, she meticulously stuck glow-in-the-dark stars to the ceiling in each of their bedrooms. If Gommy could see her handiwork tonight, she would be proud. Sam wondered if Gommy was watching the stars from Heaven by now, and if they looked more brilliant from the other side.

Gommy had been both sister and grandmother all rolled into one. Magically, she could be whatever Sam needed her to be.

Lying there alone, she thought of how sad the day had been. More than likely she would never again hear her grandmother's voice. This broke her heart, yet she didn't want to cry. Maybe she had already shed so many tears there weren't any left inside.

Without a doubt, she would miss her grandmother, but, oddly, Gommy's death didn't sting like she thought it would. There would be periods of loneliness, but tonight her mother had made it clear that she would be there doing all of the things that a mother was supposed to do.

Jillian had undergone a subtle transformation. Everything about her—though still the same—seemed softer. Even the way her words left her mouth had taken on a lighter, more positive tone. For as long as Sam could remember, her mother had been sad, but tonight, while they were driving home from the hospital, she reminded Sam of Gommy. It wasn't really that she was happy, it was more like she was calm.

As Sam thought about her mother, her mind began to race with questions.

Would her mother keep her secrets? Would she be a good listener?

Cut from the Same Cloth

Sam had always trusted her grandmother with the important things.
Could she trust her mother now?
Maybe she should just tell God. He would listen.
Isn't that what Gommy always said?
Closing her eyes, she let her mind ramble as she talked to God. After she had spilled the contents of her heart, she faced her pillow and cried herself to sleep.

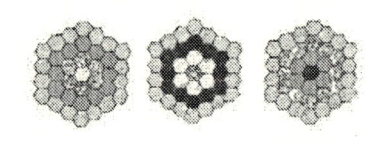

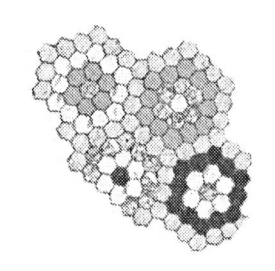

Chapter 18
The Bottom Drawer

After phoning Miss Edna to give her the news, Jillian put on her pajamas and got ready for bed. Glad that Sam was already asleep, Jillian wanted to be alone. It had been an emotional day, and she knew it wasn't quite over. The task before her would not be easy, but it had to be done. There was no choice. Even though, she dreaded what the next few days would bring, curiosity was pulling her to her mother's bedroom.

Allowing her thoughts to return to the last moments she spent with her mother, she was struck by how peacefully tender they had been. Mysteriously, her mother's coughing fits had subsided.

Replaying her mother's last words over in her head, there was no doubt what her mother had said. Her words had been perfectly clear.

"Bottom drawer."

Cut from the Same Cloth

Jillian already knew about the bottom drawer, but she had never actually seen its contents. Tonight, she would unravel another mystery.

Before heading to her mother's room, Jillian peeked in on Sam. Surely, her little girl must be exhausted, after a full day at school, then her visit with her Gommy. Sure enough, Sam was already asleep. The only sound coming from her room was the sweet sound of her snoring.

"Poor Sam," Jillian whispered, "I know this is going to be hard for you. But I won't leave you, I promise."

Blowing a kiss towards her sleeping daughter, she gently closed the door and headed to her mother's room.

Out of habit, Jillian knocked on the bedroom door. Sadly, she realized her mother would never again be waiting on the other side. Pushing the door open slowly, she entered the room as if it was a shrine. Reaching down, she felt for the small tassel that hung from the pull chain of her mother's old, white Victorian lamp and pulled it. For as long as Jillian could remember, *this* lamp had rested on *this* night stand beside *this* iron bed.

Standing in the dimly lit room, she could see the remnants of her mother's life. There were fancy glass figurines, as well as picture frames made from popsicle sticks. Gommy had never been able to throw out anything sentimental. Mementos were neatly displayed in every nook and cranny. Jillian had been in her mother's room countless times, but she had paid little attention to all of her mother's things.

Tonight, without her mother there to overshadow them, they clamored for attention. One day, she and Sam would have to go through them, but not tonight. Tonight, she had another job to do.

Laura Lea

Kneeling down before the old, cedar chest of drawers, Jillian sat on her knees. Taking a deep breath, she exhaled slowly, trying to blow away the feeling that she was a kid about to steal the cookies from the cookie jar. Grasping the drawer pulls with both hands, she gently tugged, pulling the bottom drawer open, its contents finally revealed.

The scent of cedar drifted lazily from the drawer, reminding her of the cedar hope chest Peter had given her before they were married. There, before her, she found exactly what she expected to find.

Her mother had left detailed instructions for her funeral and burial. There was also an insurance policy purchased to cover the expenses and the bill of sale for the cemetery plot. It was just like her mother to think of pre-purchasing her own cemetery plot. Gommy had even included her burial clothing.

One by one, Jillian pulled from the drawer its contents. On a piece of lavender stationery, her mother had written her instructions for carrying out her burial wishes.

She had listed the names of her four dearest friends along with their phone numbers. They had previously been given their instructions. So one call to Miss Rose and the entire affair would be carried out to her mother's specifications.

Also, written on the stationery was Gommy's favorite verse from the Bible, Genesis 28:15, along with the names of her two favorite songs from church. Included was her full name, Betty Louise Porter Black, and her date of birth, June 27, 1936.

Reading on, Jillian discovered that her mother didn't want any flowers at her funeral. Instead, she wanted donations made in her name to the local food

165

Cut from the Same Cloth

pantry where she had done volunteer work for so many years.

Wasn't that just like her mother? She was always thinking of others.

"Well, Mom, how about if I make a donation and send flowers? And guess what, Mom, for the first time in my life you have no say."

The last item written on the sheet of lavender stationery, was her mother's desire that her coffin be draped with her Grandma's Flower Garden quilt. After the funeral it was to be given to Sam. Until this moment, Jillian's curiosity had prevented her from becoming emotional, but now sitting on the floor in her mother's room, she began to weep. Finally, it was beginning to sink in. Her mother would not be coming home.

Once again, her mother had taken care of all of the details so that Jillian wouldn't have to. Jillian would need to be available for Sam. This was not a selfish act on her mother's part. Jillian knew it for what it was, it was her mother's last chance to show her daughter how to love.

For seven years, her mother had been teaching her how to love her child. She had not done it with nagging words, but rather with gentle actions. Jillian hoped Gommy knew she had been paying attention.

With tears in her eyes, she whispered, "Thank you, Mom, for everything."

Jillian knew she was ready.

Placing the stationary on the floor beside her, she pulled from the drawer a beautiful silk gown. Burying her face in it, she could feel the coolness of the fabric. It was the most beautiful garment she had ever seen. Jillian didn't recognize it from any of their shopping

Laura Lea

trips. She couldn't recall ever seeing anything like it in her mother's wardrobe.

It was definitely unique. It actually looked like it was from another country, maybe somewhere in Asia. A very simple design, it was finished off with a Mandarin collar and braided ribbon buttons.

Gommy had never worn anything like it before.

Why she had chosen it for her burial?

Jillian had no idea, but chosen it she had, and Jillian would honor her mother's wishes by making sure she wore it. It was the least she could do.

Folding the garment neatly, she placed it carefully on the rug beside her. Looking one more time into the drawer, she saw a small plastic bag. Smiling to herself, she knew its contents by heart.

There was a tube of Crushed Petals lipstick and a compact of translucent powder. Gommy wouldn't be caught dead without her makeup.

Totally exhausted, Jillian returned the items to their drawer, called Miss Rose to let her know that Gommy's time was short, then she crawled into her mother's bed and fell asleep.

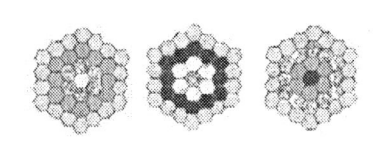

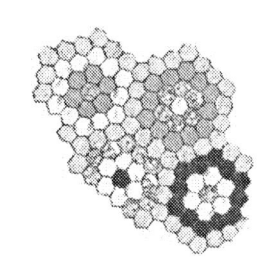

Chapter 19
Two Days Later

*T*ired of all the whispering and long faces, Sam slipped out to her tree house. She had never heard so much sad chattering in her life. For her mother's sake, she had remained quietly pleasant, but on the inside, she was screaming. The mourners had been there for hours, surely they would trickle to their cars soon. All she wanted was to have her house back.

As she and Teddy slouched on the purple bean bag chair she kept in her hideaway, the coolness of the spring rain caused her to shiver. Hugging Teddy closer, she tried to warm herself.

Rain, rain, and more rain. Sam could not understand why the weather reports kept warning about the severe drought. As she watched the gray fog cover their pasture, she wondered if the local farmers were dancing in their fields to the steady beating of the rain.

A few weeks ago, a citywide prayer meeting was held at the local football field to ask the Almighty for

Cut from the Same Cloth

rain. The drought had been so severe during the past two growing seasons that several of the local farmers were worried they might lose their farms.

As far as Sam could tell, the Almighty was in the mood to be generous. Except for a short time, two days ago, when the sun shone brightly, the rain had fallen for days. Sam knew she should be thankful for the showers, but they had done nothing to brighten her mood.

Still missing Gommy terribly, Sam had taken a small photo album and filled it with pictures her mother had given her. As each page was filled, her heart ached to see her grandmother, just one more time. Her mother had hoped the exercise would make her feel better, but it hadn't.

Right now, what she really wanted to do was lose herself in some wild, imaginary scheme, but she had been unable to summon her imagination. It had always been her way of escaping.

Gommy's death, however, had been inescapable. Consuming her thoughts, it had taken her down roads she had no desire to travel. Right now, she wanted to be somewhere else, somewhere dry, somewhere happy. No matter how hard she tried to create a mind-boggling adventure, her thoughts continued to return to her grandmother's funeral.

Having never been to a funeral, Sam had been nervous and unsure of what to expect. Now that it was all over, she couldn't help but think her grandmother would have been disappointed with the whole affair.

It had been dark and dreary. With the exception of Miss Rose and the other Perennials, everyone wore black. Even she and her mother had donned the traditional color of mourning.

Laura Lea

Sam was sure that Gommy would have been proud of her lady friends. Huddled next to each other beside the casket, they looked like a spring bouquet. They couldn't have dressed more appropriately in their bright, floral dresses. If Sam hadn't known better, she might have assumed that Gommy had personally selected their outfits. With the way those four carried on, maybe she had.

Gommy had always loved brightly colored things. If she could have been a color, she would surely have been sunflower yellow.

Today, however, had been dreary. With the exception of the Perennials, there had been nothing bright or cheery there at all.

Sam couldn't understand the whole 'no flowers' thing. Gommy loved flowers. If Sam had gotten to choose, she would have buried her grandmother in a field of pink and yellow cosmos. There, Gommy could watch her favorite flowers sway in the breeze as they reached for the sun.

Sam's favorite part of the whole funeral wasn't really part of the funeral at all. After most of the mourners were gone, Sam and her mother were joined by those who were closest to her grandmother at the grave side. Looking around the circle, she saw the faces of the people her grandmother loved most. There to pay their final respects were her mother, Mr. Bill and Miss Edna, and all of the Perennials. Even Miss Fern had come for the funeral.

Standing around the freshly mounded soil that covered her grandmother's casket, her mother passed around a small basket of tiny Cosmos seeds. Sam watched the light seeds float away as each person took a turn tossing their seeds into the air. Waiting for

Cut from the Same Cloth

her turn, she remembered a conversation she and her grandmother recently had.

She had promised Gommy that she would plant a pack of Cosmos seeds in the flower bed by the screened porch, and with all that had happened, she had never done it. Today, she would keep her promise. Reaching into the basket, she removed the remaining seeds and sprinkled them on the freshly tilled earth.

Gommy, I kept my promise, she thought. In a few short months, the seeds would sprout, yielding Gommy's favorite Cosmos blooms. Sam hoped she would approve.

Sam was a little surprised at the number of people who took the time to come by their house to pay their last respects. She had no idea her grandmother had so many friends.

She remembered feeling really sad for the Perennials. In between their trips back and forth between the kitchen and the dining room, she had seen them huddled together in tears. Gommy was the first one to die, and they were trying their best to deal with it gracefully.

They had also taken it on themselves to see to it that Gommy's funeral went off without a hitch. It was a good thing too, because people had come by the droves. They came, signed the guest book, spoke to her mother, and filled a plate with fried chicken and potato salad. Most of them slipped out quietly, taking their long faces with them.

Sam heard so many people referring to her grandmother as Louise, that she had to remind herself that Gommy and Louise were the same person.

Laura Lea

There were a few people that came because they knew Sam. Miss Molly came, and she was actually wearing real clothes and shoes. Mickey Sullivan and his mother brought a pound cake and a plate of brownies.

Mr. Bill and Miss Edna came by carrying armloads of fried chicken, baked beans, and biscuits. For the first time in Sam's recent memory, they were actually being nice to one another. Miss Edna was taking Gommy's passing especially hard, since the two of them had become close friends over the years.

The only thing Sam liked about the whole experience was the minister. He was a young man with hair so short that from a distance he looked bald. Sam was fascinated by his china blue eyes the moment she met him. They seemed to glow, and he was also very funny. Every time he saw her he would grin a silly grin and wave. Several times he had even pulled a quarter from behind her ear and given it to her.

The best thing about him was that he spoke so kindly of her grandmother. He was fairly new at the church so he didn't know Gommy all that well, but it was clear he had talked with a lot of people who did know her. Sam would never forget his words. He spoke softly, as if he was speaking of his own grandmother.

"Mrs. Louise is in Heaven now. And even though her life on earth has come to an end, her story has really just begun. As a teenager, she asked God Almighty to forgive her of her many transgressions. She accepted his forgiveness, then she chose to live her life in accordance to the Holy Scriptures. I believe Mrs. Louise has seen with new eyes all that she could only have imagined while here on earth. We know she

Cut from the Same Cloth

loved her family, her daughter, Jillian, and her precious granddaughter, Samantha."

Pausing from his message, he looked right at Jillian and Sam.

"I believe that if she could speak to you, she would want you to know that she loves her new body, that the accommodations are fabulous and that Heaven is more than she could have ever hoped for."

His words had somehow made her feel better. She still wasn't thrilled about the whole thing, but she didn't really want to cry either. When it was over, Sam realized that she didn't really know a whole lot about Gommy's God. Especially about Heaven. The whole new body thing didn't make any sense to her. Maybe she'd ask her mom, she would probably know. After all, she had lived with Gommy a whole lot longer.

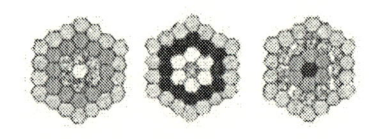

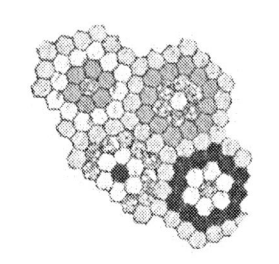

Chapter 20
Full Circle

Dinner had been simple: left-over fried chicken and vegetables from the mounds of food brought over by the Perennials and others. Sam was glad that all of the people were gone. They had been very generous, bringing enough food to feed a small army. Clearly, they were just trying to help, but Sam couldn't understand why they all brought fried chicken. She knew it was Gommy's favorite, but she wasn't there to help them eat it. More than likely there had been a sale on poultry down at Frank's Meat Market.

Sam loved fried chicken, too, but she had eaten it four times in the last three days and was ready for something different. Maybe she'd talk her mother into having pizza delivered tomorrow night. That would be nice for a change.

It had been an emotionally tiring day, so after dinner, they cleared the table and got ready for bed. Sam had been unusually quiet at dinner. The last three days had been really tough. She had been asked

Cut from the Same Cloth

to do a lot of grown up things. Deciding to check in on her daughter, Jillian tapped lightly on Sam's bedroom door.

"It's open," a voice yelled from the other side. Jillian took that to mean it was alright to enter.

"How are ya, Sammy?"

Sam wasn't sure she liked having her mom call her 'Sammy'. She had never done that before. Only Gommy had ever called her that. Not wanting to make a big deal out of something that really wasn't one, Sam answered her mother.

"I'm okay, How are you?"

"Want the truth? I'm tired...I'm tired of people I don't know telling me how sorry they are. And honestly, I'm tired of being sad."

Jillian's announcement struck a chord with Sam.

"I'm tired of the rain," Sam said with a note of disgust. "It might be easier to cheer up if the weather weren't so dreary. Mom, can I stay home from school tomorrow?" Sam asked with a tinge of hope in her voice.

"Why don't we wait until tomorrow to decide, fair enough?"

"Fair enough."

As Jillian turned to leave, Sam startled herself with her next request.

"Mom, would you sleep with me tonight?"

Jillian was touched. "Sure I will, but I need to get something first. I'll be right back."

Jillian knew this would be a perfect time to give Sam the Grandma's Flower Garden quilt. Gommy had left very clear instructions that Sam was to have it.

Jillian went to the kitchen where it was folded neatly on the counter. For a moment, she stood there looking at her mother's favorite quilt. Jillian had

Laura Lea

always admired its simple beauty. It was a testimony to the passage of time.

Her mother had taken care of it for over fifty years. Sure, it was faded and there were frayed seams, but it was still beautiful, maybe even more beautiful now that time had mellowed its bright contrasting fabrics.

Isn't that what time did to people, mellow them with age?

Jillian had always known that quilts could talk, and Gommy's was no exception. It told of a mother's love for her daughter as she headed out into the world on her own.

Realizing for the first time how much her mother was like her grandmother, Jillian gently caressed the worn fabrics. Both of them had spent their lives trying to care for their daughters, trying to teach them the value of family and sacrifice. They pushed them from the nest, *knowing* they would fly, *praying* they would soar.

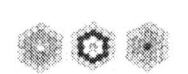

❖ ◉ ❖

*J*illian knew she was airborne. Her wings weren't strong yet, but they would be in time. She could be a good mother to Sam. After all, Louise Black had been the very best of teachers. As the tears began to spill from her eyes, Jillian whispered softly, knowing her mother could hear her.

"Thank you, Mom."

As she opened Sam's door, she found her daughter staring at the glowing stars on her ceiling.

"Sam, I brought you something. Gommy wanted you to have this."

Cut from the Same Cloth

Opening the quilt, she flung it over the bed. Even in the darkened room, Sam could make out its pattern in the glow coming from the stars mounted on her ceiling.

"I know. She asked me if I wanted her to leave it to me on the night before she went into the hospital.

"Mom, do you think Gommy knew she was going to die?"

"Oh, I don't know. She wasn't really that sick then." She paused to choose her words carefully. "You know Sam, sometimes I think people do know. I think Mom knew she was dying when we went to see her at the hospital the other night."

"Where do you think she is?"

"Where do I think she is? I don't have to think, I know exactly where she is. She's in Heaven."

"I know the minister said that, but how can you be so sure?"

"Well, Sam, Gommy loved Jesus. When she was a teenager she decided she wanted to be kind and good, just like Jesus. One time, she told me how she and her mother would get down on their knees and pray. She said they asked God for all kinds of stuff, shoes, and money for coal for their old coal burning stove."

"A what?"

"A coal burning stove."

"What's a coal burning stove?" Sam asked.

"Gommy's family was poor, so they burned coal, you know, it looks kind of like black rocks, in a big iron box. That's how they kept their house warm."

"No wonder they needed a lot of quilts."

Jillian continued on, "Gommy believed in prayer. She said there were times when they didn't have enough money for coal, and someone would just show up at their door with a bucket full of the

Laura Lea

shiniest lumps of coal they'd ever seen. But she was always clear that there was only one prayer that was really worth praying. Every night, she said, they would ask God to help them make the right choices every day."

"Mom, do you understand about the whole new body thing?"

"Boy, Sam, you really do have a lot of questions, don't you? That's a hard one. I don't think I really understand it all, but Heaven isn't like earth. It's a really special place. Everyone that goes there gets a special, new body.

"You can't take your old body to Heaven, because it's not perfect. Heaven's a perfect place. If we all showed up with these bodies, it wouldn't be perfect anymore. Have you ever heard anybody say, 'You can't take it with you'?"

"I don't think so."

"Well, just trust me. You can't take the body you use here to Heaven."

"So, Gommy has a perfect body now?" Sam quizzed

"She sure does. No more cane, no more walker."

"Do you mean her hip's well?"

"It sure is. I wonder what Gommy's new body looks like? Any guesses?"

"No, not really, but I bet she's got her hair pinned up and her lipstick on," Sam giggled.

Jillian was glad they were talking. Maybe this was helping Sam sort it all out.

"Hey, Mom, do you think she misses us?"

"I don't know. Maybe, maybe not. I'd like to think she does. But you know she hasn't been there very long, so I imagine she's still learning her way around. And don't forget, she knows a lot of folks there that

179

Cut from the Same Cloth

she hasn't seen in awhile. If I know Mom, she's doing some visiting right now."

"So, why did we do the whole funeral, cemetery thing?" Sam asked.

"Well, I guess it's because we have to do something with Gommy's old body. Remember, she didn't get to take it with her. So we have to put it somewhere for her. And she wanted us to keep it at the cemetery, she even paid for a spot a long time ago. That way, when we get sad and want to spend some time with her we can go visit her grave. I guess you could say the whole funeral and cemetery thing is for us."

"For us?" Sam questioned.

"Well, it gave us a chance to tell her goodbye. And don't forget, Gommy had a lot of friends, and they wanted to say goodbye, too."

"Maybe we can take her some flowers." Sam suggested.

"Oh, I think she'd like that. You know how much she loved flowers. You know, Sam, in a few weeks, there will be lots of little flowers starting to grow right where Gommy's buried."

"The Cosmos seeds."

"Uh-huh," Jillian said.

For a moment, they lay under the warm quilt in silence. Jillian wasn't sure if Sam was trying to think of more questions or whether she had fallen asleep. Gazing up at the star filled ceiling, she could see her own grandmother, Mimi, hanging clothes on the clothesline, the smell of bleached sheets drifting through the air. Jillian listened carefully to see if she could hear it. There it was, the unmistakable sound.

"Amazing grace, how sweet the sound...."

Laura Lea

Jillian was amazed that she could still hear the sound of her grandmother's voice as clearly as if she were in the next room. In her mind, Mimi's voice was clear and strong. She would never forget her own grandmother.

She knew that she was experiencing the promise of her grandmother's legacy. It was a legacy that had made its way to her withstanding the tests of time. It was now her turn.

She knew she was the one who would have to see that Sam understood. Feeling up to the task, she knew she had been cut from the same cloth as her mother and grandmother. The lessons of love and forgiveness were flowing through her veins.

As she lay in her daughter's bed, snuggled underneath her mother's quilt, she could just make out what she thought was a familiar patch of flannel sewn into the design.

But where had she seen it before?

All at once, she could see Peter, pushing Sam on the swing in the back yard. He was wearing a plaid, flannel shirt, this plaid flannel.

How did Mom manage to sew this into her quilt? Jillian wondered.

As her fingers traced the soft fabric she felt warm. She felt blessed. She had a second chance at being a mother. And even though she would be doing it by herself, she knew she would never be alone.

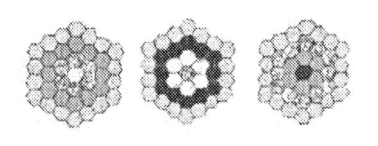

Sneak Peek due for release Winter 2006

Sneak Peek of The Last Garden

 Even with the windows raised, it was dreadfully hot. The quilt that usually draped her bed in perfect symmetry lay crumpled in a heap on the floor. Sam had spent the last few miserably, hot hours rolling from side to side in search of the cotton sheet's cool spots. Finally, at her wit's end, she rolled to the foot of the bed, turned crossways, and stared at the whirling fan blades directly overhead. Even though she could see that the blades were indeed spinning, the breeze they stirred did little to relieve the heat.

 The night was eerily quiet. Even the frogs and crickets were too hot to perform their midnight musical, preferring instead to gather someplace cool and moist. The only sound she could hear tonight was the monotonous clicking of the ceiling fan's pull chain as it rocked back and forth striking the glass light globe with each pass. Lulled into a trance by its rapping, it was easy to focus on the sea of glowing stars scattered across her bedroom ceiling.

As she continued her nightly habit of star gazing, she wondered for the umpteenth time if her grandmother was watching the real stars from heaven. Gommy had been dead since April; and it was now mid-August. Believing most of the time, that her grandmother could both see and hear everything from Heaven, Sam continued to find comfort in her daily, one-sided conversations with her heavenly grandmother.

"Gommy," she whispered as if she didn't want God to hear. "Does He let you talk up there? Do you think He might let you talk to me sometime? I miss getting to hear your voice since you moved away. I wish there was some way I could know for sure that you can hear me."

Of course, Sam knew that if it were possible her grandmother would have found a way to let her know by now.

Tired of star gazing and sweating like a pig, Sam felt positively sure this was the hottest, most miserable night of her entire life. For hours, she had counted sheep and recited the words to the Pledge of Allegiance.

She had even tried to figure out how many days she had been alive, but multiplying three digit numbers was not something she excelled at during the day with a pencil and paper in her hand, much less in the dark with nothing but her fingers and toes.

"Auuhh," she fussed, "This is crazy. It's like an oven in here."

Swinging her feet off the bed she stood quickly, causing a momentary head rush.

"Blasted air conditioner, it's August for Pete's sake. You're supposed to keep the house cool," she ranted shaking her sweat drenched curls. As her shoulder length honey colored curls slung from side-to-side, small droplets of sticky sweat splattered on her arms.

"Couldn't you have been a little more considerate? I don't know, maybe waited until October to freeze up or better yet, how 'bout January?" she mumbled, while tugging on the sleeves of her favorite Goofy tee-shirt. Once she peeled it from her tiny frame, she used it to blot the streams of sweat that were tracing down her back and chest. Even her shoulder length curls were stuck to the back of her neck.

Moving to the foot of her bed, she reached down, grabbed her quilt and slung it back onto the bed. Practically naked, she dropped to the floor in search of the clothes she dropped there before going to bed.

Thankfully, there was a full moon tonight spilling its wares into her room through two six-pane windows. Filling every available space, a hazy glow made it possible for her to see the clothes and shoes scattered about her floor.

"Bingo," she whispered, grabbing what looked like a green top and denim shorts from under her bed. Rolling over onto her back, she pulled on her shorts wiggling to get them all the way up. She felt for the tag in the neck of her tank top.

"Oops, inside out."

Not taking the time to flip the shirt she slipped it on wrong side out.

Finally dressed in dry clothes, she decided to try her luck on the screened porch. Maybe it's cooler outside. One thing led to another, and before she knew it she was planning an impromptu camp out for herself and her favorite bear, Teddy.

Excited about camping on the porch, Sam kicked it into high gear. Quickly, she trotted around her bed in the direction of a small silhouette that crouched between her bed and closet.

Surprisingly, she had been able to move about her room without arousing her mother, which was no small feat. Feeling for the knob on the top drawer of her small white night table she pulled it quickly, spilling its contents to the floor with a loud crash.

"Shhh," she hissed instinctively, raising her index finger to her pursed lips.

"Be quiet or you'll wake Mom," she told herself.

Tomorrow she'd have to ask her mother for a replacement bulb for the nightlight that plugged into the outlet by the bedroom door. Being sneaky would be a lot easier if she had even the teeniest bit of light coming from within her room. Bending down, she thumbed through the pile of miscellaneous junk that was now piled on the floor, until she felt the spiraled wire that held her diary together. Grabbing it and the only other book in the mess, she made her way to her bedroom door.

Now comes the hard part. Getting past her mother's room without calling attention to herself might be difficult. Not only was her mother a light sleeper, but on a night like this, who knew if she was even sleeping at all. Very slowly, Sam turned the glass doorknob, praying the heavy wood paneled door wouldn't tattle on her with its predictable squeal or creak.